16,840

VIDEO

CLASSROOM

GUIDE TO
VE TELEVISION

by
ON KAPLAN

Knowledge Industry Publications, Inc.
White Plains, New York

VIDEO IN THE CLASSROOM: A Guide to Creative Television
by Don Kaplan

Library of Congress Cataloging in Publication Data

Kaplan, Don.
    Video in the classroom.

    (The Video library)
    Bibliography: p.
    Includes index.
    1. Video tapes in education.   2. Educational
    games.   I. Title.   II. Series: Video library.
LB1044.7.K32   371.33′33   79-18797
ISBN 0-914236-46-6

Printed in the United States of America

CONTENTS

LIST OF TABLES

LIST OF ILLUSTRATIONS

PREFACE

Every new development of communications in the direction of the mass of people has been opposed by intellectuals of a certain stripe. I am sure that Gutenberg was denounced by the elite of his time; his device would spread dangerous ideas among the God-fearing obedient masses. The typewriter was denounced by intellectuals of the more elfin variety; its clacking would drive away the muses who apparently were accustomed to the scratching of the quill pen. The first motion pictures were denounced; they would destroy the legitimate theater. Then the sound motion picture was denounced; it would destroy the true art of the film which was pantomime.

To such critics, of course, television is destroying everything. It is destroying conversation, they tell us. Nonsense. Nonconversing families were always that way. It has, in fact, stimulated billions of conversations that otherwise would not have occurred.

It is destroying the habit of reading, they say. This is nonsense. Book sales in this country during the lifetime of general television have greatly increased and well beyond the increase in the population.

TV is debasing the use of the English language, they tell us. Nonsense. Until radio and then TV, tens of millions of people living in sharecropper cabins, in small villages on the plains and in the mountains, in the great city slums had never heard good English diction in their lives. If anything, this medium has improved the general level of diction.

You, as teachers, should say nonsense to these criticisms, too; and use television to stimulate good conversation, more reading, better diction. Consider it a basic instruction material.[1]

Television has become an integral part of the educational process—from elementary through university levels to international communications. Video teaching is receiving more (verbal) support than ever before. Education magazines regularly publish guides to watching television; journals often include descriptions of successful media programs; and reports have supported the use of video tape within the total learning environment as a teaching and research resource, as a means for solving interpersonal problems, for developing critical skills, and for overcoming basic learning problems.[2]

State arts agencies and advocacy groups support it, yet little effort is spent on developing materials for doing—not just watching—television. Whether it is a modest portapak or an elaborate color studio, most schools already have some video equipment...but having the equipment does not guarantee that teachers know how to apply it, and supertechnical results do not mean that students understand the creative process behind it. A resistance has been noted by William Harley of the National Association of Educational Broadcasters:

> By and large schools have been slow to adopt media education as part of teacher education. You can produce the finest program in the world, but the real test is in how it is utilized in the classroom. These programs are not intended to stand alone; they must relate to the total educational environment.[3]

Recommendations cannot be put into effect until the need is recognized and until recently teacher resistance has limited the development of utilization programs. Even where faculty support is strong, few programs have been created that relate the medium to the total educational environment. As LeBaron and Kamis note in the *Elementary School Journal,* "Student use...is still rare for reasons that have little to do with technology. The tools are seldom used because few educators have given serious thought to developing ways in which the school curriculum can be enriched by pupil-created television."[4]

Video in the Classroom has been designed to help teachers initiate "pupil-created" television in the schools. It is intended to meet the needs of teachers new to the medium, those with modest media means and media professionals seeking creative uses. It focuses on video tape as a tool for building skills and techniques at the very core of learning, for achieving professional standards (a "good" production does not necessarily mean professional looking results, but the amount of learning achieved through the process), and for reaching fundamental educational goals using the most economical means.

Basic production techniques have been included for the novice; more elaborate mechanical matters have been avoided...there are many books already available on the subject but none that deal entirely with video learning in the various subject areas. Instructional development specialists and media support personnel will find the text valuable for preparing teacher-training and in-service courses, and will be able to use the activities as resources for helping other instructors develop materials in their own fields—e.g., documenting a sociological report; dramatizing future events (social studies); or demonstrating career opportunities to handicapped students. Equally important is *Video in the Classroom's* value as a resource for teachers *outside* the media fields: the history, art, English, speech, or physical education teacher will find ways of integrating video tape into his or her classroom to reinforce and stimulate different areas of learning.

Chapters can be used sequentially (moving from introductory exercises to more interdisciplinary applications), independently, in combination with other chapters, as separate courses of study, or integrated within different subject areas. (A subject index has been included to help the reader locate activities for particular disciplines.) Both "humanistic" and "academic" approaches have been emphasized throughout. Taping interviews, seeing oneself on television, sharing feelings with others, and producing programs by and for other students will help build trust, more positive self images, more positive attitudes toward learning and students who are "different." There are sections on video games, nonverbal communication and self-analysis; there are suggestions for special graphic effects, for analyzing TV commercials and for future studies. Elementary, junior high, high school and university instructors will all be able to directly use those activities identified at the various levels and should have no difficulty modifying activities at other levels to meet their students' needs.

The greatest significance of video tape in the classroom is its flexibility and adaptability —its power for reinforcing concepts already being taught and stimulating interest in those yet to be encountered. The equipment is affordable, the rudiments can be learned in less than a day and the need is being recognized. According to Anthony Prete in *Media and Methods:*

> A recent survey funded by the Corporation for Public Broadcasting and the National Center for Education Statistics shows that some 15 million of the nation's 45 million elementary and high school students regularly receive instruction from teachers who use television in their classrooms. Instructional TV is available in 74% of all classrooms (the good news), is regularly used by 32% of the teachers (the bad news), and only 17% of them are trained in its use (the really bad news).
>
> In the sensitive area of citizen attitudes toward education, there are also encouraging signs. A recent Roper Organization survey—also funded by CPB—shows that 72.1% of the public approved of students watching TV in school, 58.6% endorsed assigning television programs as homework, and (budget committees take note) 59.5% supported the use of tax dollars for instructional television. The survey also showed (evaluation teams take note) that teachers who use television in the classroom are regarded by the public as progressive, industrious, and creative.
>
> So the resources are there, the interest is there, the encouragement is there, even the funds are—or could be—there. All that's lacking, at least in the schools that have TV but don't use it, is initiative.[5]

Creative uses of the medium in schools should be emphasized over startling displays of video virtuosity, as well as active learning over passive and techniques developed for delivering clear messages through a minimum of media hardware. "Television can be a tremendous teaching tool but the medium must be taken more advantage of..."[6] Herewith, the initiative, and a method for taking that advantage.

Notes

1. Eric Sevareid, "TV destroys reading? 'Nonsense'," *Instructor*, March 1978.

2. *Coming to our senses: The Significance of the Arts for American Education* (New York: McGraw-Hill, 1977).

3. William G. Harley, President, National Association of Educational Broadcasters, in *Coming to our senses*, p. 199.

4. John LeBaron and Louise Kanus, "Child-created Television in the Inner City," *Elementary School Journal* 75 (April 1975), p. 409.

5. Anthony Prete, "In Focus" column, *Media and Methods*, October 1978.

6. Ann Hill, Past President, American Theatre Association, in *Coming to Our Senses*, p. 199.

ACKNOWLEDGEMENTS

Special thanks to Jim Lerman, President of the Metropolitan Center for Educational Development, and Jack Herman, Director of AV Educational Communications for District 6 (New York City) for their support and resources; Joe Fury, teacher-in-charge, I.S.233 (New York City) for the opportunity to try out new and reinforce old ideas; Rita Allen and Rick Moran, Photo Associates News Service, and Jackie Katz, for their time and photographic talents; Emma Cohn, New York Public Library Young Adult Services (Donnell Center) for both moral and culinary support; and Ellen Lazer, my editor at Knowledge Industry Publications, for her guidance and, especially, her patience.

I am grateful for permission to reprint sections of the following:

Remote Control: Television and the Manipulation of American Life, by Frank Mankiewicz and Joel Swerdlow. Reprinted by permission of Quadrangle/Times Books, © 1978 by Frank Mankiewicz and Joel Swerdlow.

"In Focus" column, by Anthony Prete, from the October 1978 issue of *Media and Methods* magazine, © 1978 by North American Publishing Company.

"TV destroys reading? 'Nonsense'," by Eric Sevareid, as quoted in "TV as a Teacher's Ally" from the March 1978 issue of *Instructor* magazine.

INTRODUCTION

It is not smart to ignore the most significant force in our society. Alert yourself to the medium. Determine what is worth communicating. Get thinkers together with creators. Team with professionals and make a program yourself. Make TV deliver.[1]
Nicholas Johnson

With the advent of television, for the first time in history, all aspects of animal and human life and death, of societal and individual behavior have been condensed on the average to a 19 inch diagonal screen and a 30 minute time slot.[2]
Jerzy Kosinski

Television is the Great American Dream Machine. Through it "people are now reached, persuaded and informed more extensively than every before....[TV is] a machine to manufacture reassurance for troubled Americans ... to disconnect the audience from uncomfortable realities, to lull it on a sea of gentle inconsequence—and then to sell it deodorant."[3] So says Robert MacNeil, quoted in *Coping with Television*. Addressed "To Whom It May Concern," the Dream Machine presents a world where the most serious problems can be sprayed, washed, scrubbed, rinsed, and foamed away. It jabbers for hours at anyone who will listen, and ignores human contact. It affects our everyday lives in ways we are not even aware of, yet for the most part we have chosen to passively absorb its dreams and allow them to spread over us like margarine.

Medium: an intervening substance...through which a force acts or an effect is produced; an agency, means, or instrument

Television has been accused of accomplishing everything from creating "vidiots"[4] to destroying the American family; from dictating what we should eat to how we should mate.

Studies are readily available on the psychological and sociological impacts of the medium, the evils of children's television and the dangers of commercial broadcasting. Less information is available on transforming those criticisms into actions, and on identifying projects which facilitate the change from passive watching to humanistic and real-life learning. The critical focus has been on looking at, not *doing* television. Since mass media involve a flow of information in one direction only, the emphasis needs to be shifted from idle receivers to informed transmitters.

Using a video tape recorder (VTR) in the classroom may not change the fact of commercial programming, but it will help students develop an awareness of what is coming into their homes, directly influencing their lives.

Medium: a liquid with which pigments are mixed for application

The first channels of communication were inefficient and severely limited by time and space. Messages arrived individually, evolved slowly, and became more complex as a result of gradual change. Mass media transmit their messages instantly and those messages are as perishable as the shows of the new season. We do not take the time to stop, to look at every perception; we reject any product that is not "brand new." Images arrive from all directions at once; they assault us every day in nonlinear patterns and we often stop sensing in defense. The television camera, similar to other recording devices, has the ability to frame our impressions of the world. It forces us to see a movement, hear a bit of dialogue, explore a fragment of time. It is a living genre painting, a photographic journal, an electronic note-taker. It can widen and deepen our understanding of what it means to be alive, equip us with new ways of analyzing and considering the constant flow of images, and enable us to communicate feelings that might not otherwise be expressed.

By crystallizing and condensing information into a single audiovisual image, TV heightens our skills in observation, our attention to detail and our capacity for abstraction and development of the fullest potential of a single idea.

Medium: a manifestation of some alleged supernatural agency

Few people can ignore a camera. Its magic is irresistible. Set up a tripod or use a portapak on the street and you're certain to draw a crowd; try to pass a monitor in a window display without glancing over your shoulder to look at yourself.

The use of video involves children in ways few other materials can. They respond naturally to a medium they have grown up with, shared with their friends, and on which they are natural "authorities." TV commands their attention, generates excitement, increases attendance, and promotes greater retention of skills. Maximum learning can occur when students are actively engaged in planning, producing and evaluating programs of their own creation.

Unfortunately, aside from schools where special media classes exist, video equipment is generally used as an "audiovisual aide"—a many-tentacled appendage to learning kept under the guard of the media squad, carried in on occasion to liven up a lesson.

Once the equipment is demystified, however, it becomes as familiar and useful a tool as the ordinary chalkboard. Teachers who are concerned about being replaced by the Dream

Machine are needed more than ever to operate it, produce programs, direct student projects, and teach the new communications. Video can be used to improve instruction, emphasize a lesson, reduce preparation time, free teachers to give individual attention to more students, and establish interdisciplinary relationships. Motivation and student/teacher interaction increase (contributing to a positive classroom atmosphere) as teachers become involved in the magic of the camera through production and discussion. Instead of being unidirectional, instructional lessons can be designed to encourage *students* to share their experiences with each other, and to create lessons that are effective and satisfying.

Medium: the element in which an organism has its natural habitat; one's environment, surrounding things, conditions or influences

With a portapak, students become explorers; they investigate, research, organize, and document their findings. Rather than inhibit learning and real life experiences, the process helps students develop attitudes of responsibility for their own actions and interactions with others since any production requires the cooperation of a number of people. Student producers schedule activities and meet deadlines; learn to care for equipment; develop leadership and communication skills; learn to collaborate in order to achieve a common goal; and develop standards and attitudes of responsibility toward their audience. At the end of the process, students continue to learn by modifying their work and hearing the criticisms of others.

The portapak moves students through the school and community, heightening awareness of the world around them. The user can look more closely at the environment and discriminate between fact and opinion. He or she can communicate with older adults and younger children and speak with professionals and discover the realities of business, the arts and a variety of jobs. *The process of "doing" produces awareness of the illusions and manipulations behind the screen and enables examination of the realities occurring in front.*

Medium: the substance by which specimens are displayed or preserved; a nutritive substance...in or upon which microorganisms are grown for study.

When used to stimulate rather than patch up areas of the curriculum, video becomes an organic part of the educational process: it neither supplements nor supplants the traditional subjects. It enables students who have language difficulties to express themselves and communicate visually while simultaneously developing their research, oral, reading and writing skills. Taping encourages experimentation and divergent learning—any number of approaches can be tried, mistakes corrected immediately, and solutions chosen from a variety of alternatives.

Students need to understand the new media, what the equipment does and how it affects what they see in both linear and nonlinear modes of expression. Equally important is what students *do* with the camera—how they use it to form and shape their ideas. Our educational concerns should be with both methods and messages, the ways of actively engaging students in thinking, learning, producing and evaluating through media.

Video tape is an effective teaching and research resource. Get the equipment and make some magic! The medium may be the message, but it is prime time we took some responsibility for that message.

Notes

1. Nicholas Johnson, "What Do We Do About Television?" in *Coping with Television*, ed. Joseph Littell (Evanston: McDougal, Littell and Company, 1973), p. 205.

2. Jerzy Kosinski, "TV Children," in *Mass Media and the Popular Arts,* ed. Frederic Rissover and David C. Birch (New York: McGraw-Hill, 1972), p. 170.

3. Robert MacNeil, as quoted in *Coping with Television,* p. 8.

4. John M. Culkin, *Films Deliver,* ed. Anthony Schillaci and John M. Culkin (New York: Citation Press, 1970), p. 19.

1

Please Stand By...
How Video Works

...what you're experiencing is process. And the same process would be with clay, paint—anything. In this case the material just happens to be the electron.[1]

Gene Youngblood

Many curriculum areas are incorporated into a television production. Language skills, research, organization, scriptwriting, speaking, listening, art, music, and the interpersonal skills necessary to complete a video tape contribute to students' social, emotional and academic learning. Students do not have to become professionals in the media fields to benefit from video production activities; mastering technical skills helps underachievers develop feelings of accomplishment. Knowing why television works—how an image or sound gets from one place to another—enables students to use equipment more confidently, with greater sense of control under varying conditions in the field or studio. (Classroom or professional studio productions have the advantage of allowing the crew almost total control over the technical elements of videotaping; location or impromptu shootings have an immediate and spontaneous quality difficult to achieve in a studio, but the environment is more difficult to control.) Understanding what can be achieved under favorable conditions will enable students to work under adverse conditions, and help them think ahead when taping spontaneously.

Depending upon the equipment, a gizmo here may provide more control over the input of sound; an extra knob there may provide more image clarity. The explanations and suggestions in this and subsequent chapters are directed primarily toward users of the portapak—the VTR (video tape recorder) most likely to be found in schools. The basic functions of all cameras, decks and monitors, whatever the brand, are identical; they all feed on and feed back information in the form of aural and visual images. If your specialized controls are not included here, they can probably be found in the technical manuals listed in the bibliography.

BASIC VIDEO EQUIPMENT: Camera, VTR, monitor, AC/DC convertor.

Equipment Selection

Video is available in several formats: 2 inch quadraplex (professional studio decks using four video heads) with transverse scan (the video information is recorded in bands that are almost perpendicular to the length of the tape); disc formats (for slow motion effects and instant replay); 1 inch widths (providing broadcast quality at a lower cost and used primarily in institutions); three-quarter inch, half, and quarter-inch widths. Half-inch is the most popular format, combining moderate cost, flexibility and quality of image. (Usually, the wider the tape, the better the quality, since more information can be stored on it.)

Because video technology is advancing so rapidly, no attempt will be made in this book to detail the manufacturers and various formats available: by the time you understand the system, another is ready to replace it. The basic techniques outlined in this book will continue to be appropriate whatever the technology. However, a few suggestions will help facilitate the purchase of equipment and the transition from older to newer equipment.

The standard half-inch, open reel black and white formats in use during the 1970s are being replaced by color video cassette systems. Since VCRs (video cassette recorders) became practical during the mid to late 1970s, two formats—Beta and Video Home System (VHS)—have become the most popular. Unfortunately, VHS and Beta systems are not compatible with each other (they differ in both recorder and cassette design); even within the same format, different models are often incompatible.

Several factors should be considered when purchasing equipment: compatability (will you be able to exchange tapes with other schools?), construction and precision of operation, amount of recording time available, and audio dub capability (some recorders do *not* have this). Since it takes the heads a few moments to achieve maximum speed, stopping and starting the tape (open reel or cassette) normally produces a roll or glitch: by allowing the tape to run five to 10 seconds at the beginning and end of a scene, the glitch can be avoided. The amount of roll depends upon the equipment: some of the newer VCRs have an automatic backspacing editing system which backs up the tape slightly when the camera is stopped, preventing the glitch from occurring. Most of the newer decks can edit with an editing control accessory; special cables or adapter boxes are necessary when connecting a portable to a deck-type VCR, since portables do not have enough inputs or outputs. The basic functions of open reel and cassette equipment remain the same, although some controls may be more convenient on VCRs (e.g., the RF adapter is usually built in). Industrial half-inch systems offer memory access and remote control as well.

As lighter, smaller, more rugged and less expensive equipment becomes available, the older portable color video cameras will also become outdated. In general, color cameras are heavier, more complex and more difficult to operate than black and white cameras. Most require a separate Camera Control Unit, and a white balance contol and color temperature control must be set for color correction. Several high power lights must be used for indoor shooting to achieve optimum clarity and color. (Fluorescent and incandescent lights do not contain the full spectrum of colors as sunlight does; mixing indoor with outdoor lighting presents additional problems owing to the difference in color temperatures.) Cameras generally have a built-in microphone, zoom lens (ratios vary) and an optional electronic viewfinder (producing

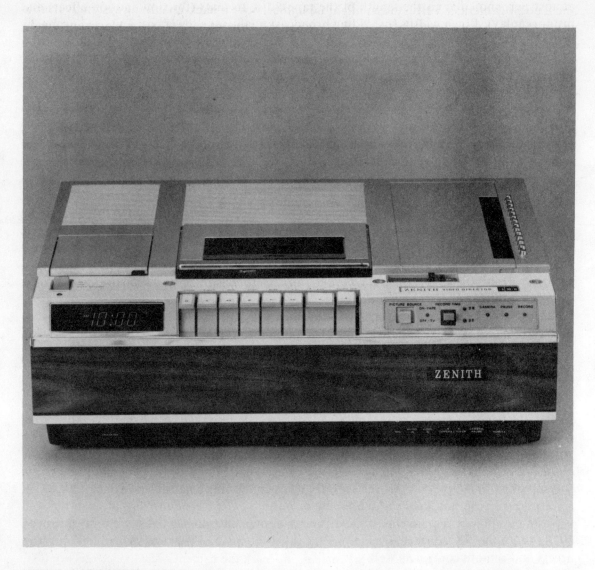

VIDEO CASSETTE RECORDER in half-inch Beta format. Reel-to-reel equipment is gradually being replaced by cassettes, which are much easier to handle. (Courtesy Zenith.)

black and white images); some have an AGC (Automatic Gain Control) or ALC (Automatic Light Control).

A portable Beta system might provide longer recording time, automatic controls, audio dub and a color camera; a VHS system might be lighter, have a back-up editing system, variable speed frame search, freeze frame and slow motion capability, but use a black and white camera. The only way to choose a new system is to ask questions, read professional and consumer literature, and purchase the equipment that best meets your needs.

There are a number of publications that offer helpful background information on video equipment and technology. They include *Video in Libraries* (White Plains, NY: Knowledge Industry Publications, Inc., 1980), *The Video Primer* (New York: Links Books, 1974), *Practical Video* (White Plains, NY: Knowledge Industry Publications, Inc., 1978) and *Television Production* (New York: McGraw-Hill, 1979). Other sources of information are various home video handbooks and journals, plus the equipment manufacturers' brochures themselves.

Transmission and Reception

As you read this page, your eyes start at the upper left hand corner, scan horizontally across the printed line, jump diagonally down to the beginning of the next line and so on until all the lines are read. When you reach the bottom of the page your eyes jump up to start a new one. The TV camera operates in a similar manner, scanning individual lines of (electronic) information to form a cumulative image, shutting off as it moves from one line to the next and coordinated by a "sync" pulse. In North America one picture is composed of 525 lines, a number small enough to be unobtrusive, yet large enough to allow for sufficient detail. (Each line contains approximately 500 separate illumination points.) The camera reads half the lines during one scan (or field), then jumps up and reads the remaining (alternate) lines during the second scan; the total of both fields ($262\frac{1}{2}$ + $262\frac{1}{2}$) equals one frame, or picture. Unlike movies where each frame can be clearly seen by holding up the film, the TV picture is stored electronically on tape and cannot be seen unless played back through video equipment. A series of thirty frames per second, passing quickly before the eye, creates the illusion of movement.

Behind the lens of the camera is a vidicon tube. A small "gun" in back shoots a stream of electrons onto the photoelectrical surface covering the front of the tube. Where light hits the surface (reflected from an object and entering through the camera's lens) electrons are lost, creating an effect similar to writing a message with your finger on an iced piece of glass. The beam from the gun scans the surface, fills in the space left by the lost electrons, and "reads" the picture. The more light that hits the surface, the stronger the electronic reaction. Light that has been converted into electronic impulses (video signals) is then fed into the VTR which further converts the signals into magnetic impulses. These impulses are recorded on iron oxide particles adhering to the plastic video tape. The particles remain in a random pattern until changed by an electromagnet (the head), proportionate to the signal received, which enables the sound and picture to be stored on and retrieved from the tape.

During playback the entire process is reversed. Magnetic impulses (particles aligned by the magnet in a similar manner to aligning iron filings on a piece of paper with a magnet held below) are converted back into electrical signals, then back into light. The picture tube acts as an inverted camera with a "gun" shooting electrons onto the tube's photoelectrical surface, line by line and field by field, coordinated by the sync pulse, causing light to be given off in the tube in direct proportion to light entering the camera. The intensity of the beam registers as light or dark (each of the 500 dots per line glows from white through various shades of gray to black depending upon the electronic charge). When there is no input, the deflected beam creates 525 blank lines (called the "raster").

Commercial television (open circuit) is transmitted by an antenna and broadcast through the air using radio frequencies (RF). The frequencies are picked up by a rooftop antenna, carried to television receivers in the home (tuned in to the broadcast antenna's wavelength) and reconverted into light. Open circuit broadcasting has its limitations. Signals lose strength as distance increases, can be blocked by natural (mountains, the curve of the earth) or man-made obstacles (skyscrapers which reflect the signals causing "ghosts" or double images) and are subject to environmental interference. RF signals are transmitted through the Very High Frequency (VHF) wave—the same band shared by police cars, FM radio stations and several other television channels, creating additional opportunities for interference. Community Antenna Television (CATV), developed to avoid the problems associated with RF broadcasting and resulting in clearer reception, uniform transmission, and minimal inter-channel adjustment, uses a coaxial cable to carry amplified signals from the base of a high antenna (picking up signals from distances over a hundred miles away) along trunk lines through specific geographic areas, into feeder lines, and finally drop lines to individual television sets. The cost of laying cables, amplifying signals and broadcasting is paid for by customers subscribing to CATV. Unless tapes are broadcast by CATV, your students will be using Closed Circuit Television (CCTV)—the direct transmission of signals from source (camera) to receiver (monitor) through cables connected to both.

There are two methods for playing back tapes or seeing live broadcasts: a *monitor*, which accepts direct video signals from the deck, or the home television set *(receiver)*, which accepts broadcast RF signals or direct signals when modified through the use of an RF adapter. Before playing a tape, be certain the monitor (or receiver) is working; set the controls for brightness and contrast, watch for glare and reflections, and adjust room light. Under ideal viewing conditions, the monitor is placed four to six feet from the floor and tilted down 30° from the student closest to the monitor. The horizontal viewing angle should not exceed 45° or distortion will occur.

Plugging In

Everything goes into or out from the deck. The camera is connected by a coaxial cable, secured to the deck's *Camera* input by tightening the plug's outer shell. If the built-in microphone is used, no further connection is necessary. An external microphone plugs into the microphone jack, and headphones (by a miniplug) into the appropriately labeled jack. Plug the VTR into the wall if it is a studio deck; on the portapak, plug in the battery or AC/DC converter. If using a television receiver rather than a monitor, plug one end of the RF converter into the deck *(RF Out)*, attach the leads on the other end to the two antenna screws on the television, switch the converter to *VTR,* and tune in the proper channel on the set (varies by geographic location). On the portapak, the *Camera* input is the same plug used to connect the monitor. (Until students learn how to set up the equipment, label parts and display a chart showing what goes where—e.g. A to A, B to B, etc. See Table 1.1.)

TABLE 1.1:Operating Video Equipment

Record

- Connect camera to camera input on deck (10 to 10 pin cable on the portapak); switch deck to *Camera*.

- Connect power source *(External Power In)*.

- Connect external microphone to microphone input; connect headphones via miniplug.

- Thread tape (heads should not be moving), check path, turn power on and run for a few feet. (Portable models have a half-hour capacity; studio decks, one-hour tape capacity.)

- Uncap lens.

- Put deck in standby position (press *Record* and *Forward* buttons together; the heads are now in motion.) Allow ten seconds to warm up.

- View picture on in-camera monitor (a miniature TV set) and set shot; adjust aperture, zoom in to close-up to focus, and zoom out to desired shot.

- Monitor audio on headphones.

- Set index to 000.

- Press camera trigger to record (a red light will appear in the viewfinder), roll for a count of five before starting, allowing heads to achieve maximum speed. Press again to stop.

- Adjust tracking for clear, noise-free picture.

Playback

- On the portapak, unplug the camera cable and connect the monitor with an 8 (monitor) to (VTR) pin cable. If using a receiver, connect the RF adapter. The in-camera monitor can be used in the field.

- Rewind (stop, rewind, stop) and play (press *Play*).

- Switch monitor to *VTR*; adjust for brightness, contrast, horizontal and vertical stability.

The tape follows a path from the supply reel to the erase head, then (depending upon the model) past the video heads (record/playback) and audio/control track head to the take-up reel. (The tape path is uncomplicated. However, be certain the tape passes *between* the rubber roller and capstan.) Two video heads rotate on a bar and protrude from the rim of the drum assembly; the tape passes over the heads in the opposite direction to achieve the necessary "writing" speed while enabling the tape and heads to move at practical speeds. In helical scan recording (half-inch) the tape angles down in a helix pattern, and around the drum in an omega-shaped pattern allowing the heads to record over most of the tape width. The pattern appears as long slanted lines, with space at the top and bottom for the audio and control tracks. Each head records or plays back one field each time it touches the tape. (One-inch helical formats use only one head with the tape wrapping around most or all of the drum.)

Differences between Film and Television

Both television and film use similar narrative devices and compositional techniques. Camera lenses are basically the same; film can be recorded on video tape and video tape on film. *Methods of transmission* are the only basic differences between them as means of communication, but an examination of those differences in Table 1.2 reveals the unique potential of each.

TABLE 1.2: Film versus Television

Film	Television
Recorded and transmitted by optical means.	Recorded and transmitted by electronic means.
Crisp image—harder, sharper, more stable.	Soft image due to scan lines. Subject to rolls, slides, jumps, glitches.
Larger and easier to watch; can capture extreme long shots filled with action.	Smaller, with different screen proportions and loss of detail.
Uses one screen only for viewing.	Several screens can be looped together at once.
Images register on light-sensitive film, are stored on plastic film (permanently fixed by chemical means) and reproduced by projecting light through fixed images.	Light is transformed into electronic energy, stored on magnetic tape and transformed electronically back into light.
Requires different equipment for recording, developing, and projecting; requires darkened room for viewing.	Records and plays back on same equipment; can be seen in daylight on any television set.
Color better, more expensive to use; color film necessary.	Color poorer, less expensive to use; same tape used for color and black and white.
Cannot transmit images without using film.	Can transmit images without recording through a closed circuit set-up.
Needs special lighting and lighting measurements indoors; often needs lighting outdoors.	Can record with available light under most conditions.
Only one person can see the actual image while it is being filmed.	Many people can see the actual image on monitors while it is being recorded.
One camera usually shoots each scene many times from several angles; a fraction of the	Two or three cameras used simultaneously; most editing done "in camera" with a switcher.

Film	Television
film is acutally used. The entire film is assembled outside the camera.	Assembled by scenes rather than shots. All of the tape is used.
Manual and optical editing—precise, easy.	Electronic editing (difficult to edit manually) with the ability to preview splices. Less precise.
Outside processing—time-consuming and expensive.	Instantaneous transmission—can be transmitted live or played back in minutes.
Sound is synchronized later on magnetic tape then transferred to film on optical soundtracks—expensive and time consuming.	Automatically synchronizes picture and sound electronically.
Microphones almost always hidden from view.	Visible microphones considered natural in several formats.
Camera needs to be isolated from microphones: mechanics are noisy.	Mechanically quiet.
Film more expensive and can be used only once. A 400 foot roll of 16mm film lasts for 11 minutes.	Tape less expensive and can be used many times: approximately 200 head passes. More continuous playing time available—30 minutes on portable decks, 60 on studio decks, allowing for lengthy documentation.
More expensive to operate.	Less expensive to operate.
Animation easier, popular, and less expensive.	Animation difficult and rarely used.
More formal (go to a theater, buy a ticket, sit in a darkened room with many other people, concentrate, watch and listen without talking, leave). Illusionary and manipulative quality.	More casual and intimate (part of the home environment, entering and leaving our awareness). More immediate and participatory. Reality quality.
Not always practical—time consuming and difficult to set up; requires a crew of at least two people.	More flexible and spontaneous; easier to operate (one person can record picture and sound at the same time). Instant evaluation and correction capability allow for greater experimentation.
Easy, established distribution.	Distribution becoming easier as more people acquire cassette players.
Product viewed many times by small audiences.	Broadcast product viewed relatively few times by mass audiences. Commercial products are short-lived, requiring a constant supply of new material.

The availability of video tape has enabled filmmakers to experiment more freely and economically than before. The portable VTR can be taken on location by filmmakers with little effort and scenes can be blocked, taped and viewed without delay. Actors and actresses do not have to wait to see rushes to evaluate their performances. Different treatments, camera angles, shots, and compositions can be tested and viewed on site; natural background sounds recorded for future use; scenes easily modified and even removed; and directors assured that the intended feeling is communicated before a single foot of film is shot. The video version serves as a model for script, timing, camera viewpoint and sequence, resulting in experimentation and spontaneity otherwise restricted by expensive film budgets. When the film is actually made, fewer takes are necessary, resulting in substantial financial savings. Film sequences can then be transferred back to tape for use as a work print (electronic editing is easier to correct than optical editing).

Lenses

Both television and movie cameras use four basic types of lenses:

- normal (25mm focal length)

- wide angle (less than 25mm—increases distance; creates the illusion of objects being further apart and away than they are; produces a broader, deeper, sharper picture)

- telephoto (longer than 25mm—limits depth of field to the subject focused on; exaggerates camera movement making it impractical for hand-held situations; narrows the angle, compresses distance and creates the illusion of objects being closer than they are)

- zoom (changes focal length from telephoto to wide angle, usually in a 4:1 ratio)

Most television cameras have a zoom lens, allowing the cameraperson to simulate dollies and use a variety of focal lengths in smooth succession. (Focal length is determined by the distance between the optical center point of the lens and area upon which the image is focused.)

The amount of light hitting the tube is controlled by an iris, opening and closing to allow in greater or smaller amounts of light, functioning in a manner similar to the human eye. The various openings (apertures) are referred to by f-stops: the higher the f-stop the smaller the opening. (The usual range is f1.8 to f16 or 22, with f5.6 as a median point.) By turning the ring on the lens barrel, the picture will brighten or darken as each stop clicks into place. (Do not set the f-stops. They are only intended as a guide. Use your eyes to achieve the best image. How high or low an f-stop would be necessary for indoor shooting? For shooting in bright sunlight? Which f-stop is necessary for your own classroom?)

To focus with a zoom lens, zoom in to a close-up (longest focal length), focus (using the focusing ring on the lens barrel) and zoom back out to the focal length you want to use. The subject will remain in focus for that shot; however, if either the camera or subject moves, the tape will have to be stopped to refocus or the cameraperson will have to "follow focus" while zooming (turn both zoom and focusing rings simultaneously).

Try arranging students in different patterns to determine which can help avoid the use of follow focus (place subjects equally distant from the lens), and which can make its use easier.

The area that will be in focus depends upon the camera/subject distance, lens used and size of the aperture. Depth can be increased by stopping down the lens (reducing the size of the aperture but necessitating more light on the subject, increasing the camera-to-subject distance or using a shorter lens. To observe depth of field, arrange students in a single diagonal line receding from the camera. Compare depth of field using a normal lens to that of a wide-angle lens (longer and deeper depth of field), and then telephoto lens (shallow depth of field). Repeat the exercise, increasing and decreasing the aperture (the higher the f-stop, the greater the depth of field). Narrow depth of field can be used to isolate subjects (e.g., in crowds); exaggerated depth of field can extend time or represent futility (a subject continues to walk or run but does not appear to be moving any closer).

Lighting

Unlike film where even outdoor shooting requires additional light, the black and white video camera needs little light—natural and ordinary classroom lighting are generally sufficient. Pick up the camera and explore; test the equipment under different conditions in and outside the school, identifying where you can shoot with natural light and where light needs to be added. (Since the picture can be seen on the in-camera monitor, these experiments do not have to be taped unless they will be played back for subsequent analysis.)

The basic purposes of lighting are to illuminate and to improve picture quality through the appropriate amount and placement of light. Lighting is used dramatically for composition and mood,[2] to achieve a sense of reality and depth (by modeling and separating foreground subjects from background subjects), and for cosmetic purposes (highlighting or diminishing physical qualities). Before spending what remains of your budget on electrical contraptions, find out what lighting equipment and attachments are really necessary (flood and spot lights, scoops, gaffers tape, a few clamps and pic stands should be sufficient) and consider how much can actually be plugged into the room you are using as a studio (available wattage).

Never aim the camera directly into the sun or a bright light—this will cause a permanent burn in the tube and necessitate a costly replacement.[3] Shooting near windows can present a problem. Try aiming the camera at students standing against a wall, then near the windows. What was clearly lit before will now require a higher f-stop (smaller lens opening). Moving from a poorly to a brightly lit area may also cause "flare-ups" (areas of bright light) and unidentifiable silhouettes (formerly identifiable as students) due to excessive light behind the students. Add a key light or zoom in as closely as possible to the subject—see below. When indoor lighting becomes necessary, keep it simple. Add one key light and a side light to start. Use light to clarify anything that is important, that needs to be seen (faces, objects, areas of the set, visual materials), for dramatic effect (shadows, spotlighting, and fades created by opening and closing the aperture) and to achieve an image with good contrast. Consider each setup in terms of intensity (measured in lumens—the total amount of light which one candle emits), direction and quality (soft/hard) of light. Too much light will wash out a picture, flattening and fading it; too little will add dimension and detail, but can also result in a noisy (snow pattern) picture. Evaluate the setups by looking for unnatural shadows, halos (too much or improperly focused backlight), hot spots (key lighting too high), and for even lighting on the subjects. (The source of the problem can be pinpointed by turning lights off one at a time, or by "flagging"—waving a hand in front of each light.)

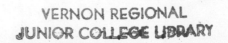

As students become more familiar with the possibilities of video, they will want to use the techniques described below to enhance their productions. Remember that the image you see in the camera is the same one transmitted to the screen. Judge with your eyes, not always by the rules.

Types of light

Lights (Table 1.3) are characterized by the direction from which they illuminate the subject or set. Light rarely comes from directly above or straight across (this would create unnatural shadows). Place lights so that they reach the subject from approximately 45° angles, unless a special effect is desired. Below are descriptions of kinds of light:

TABLE 1.3: Types of Light

a) *Key (or Primary) light.* A spotlight: the main source of illumination for the subject and first light to be set (add one or two, depending upon what is being lit). As a modeling light, it casts shadows, builds form and highlights the subject. Placement: above (determined by the physical contours of the subject) and to one side of the subject, illuminating the subject at an angle between thirty and forty-five degrees. Highly directional.

b) *Rim (or Back) light.* The secondary source of illumination for the subject. Another modeling light, used for contrast and to develop a three-dimensional quality (separating subjects from background). Placement: a spotlight hung on a stand or wall behind and above the subject, opposite the camera, aimed at the subject's head and shoulders (highlighting these areas) at a steeper angle than the key and fill lights.

c) *Fill (or Side) light.* A general floodlight (scoop or brood) which fills in harsh, unnatural shadows created by the modeling lights. (Some shadows are necessary—try eliminating all shadows and observe the effect.) Placement: at the same angle as the key but from the other side; can be aimed directly at the set or bounced off the ceiling or walls. Soft, diffuse, and nondirectional. The combination of key, rim and fill light is referred to as "three-point lighting" and comprises the basic lighting plan for nondramatic action.

d) *Background lights.* High or low key, used to illuminate the set behind the subject(s). Background lights should be balanced with the three-point arrangement.

e) *Accent lights.* Spotlights added for highlights, originating from behind or from the sides.

f) *Cross light.* A modeling light, crossing the subject, originating from the side of the set.

TABLE 1.4: Lighting Instruments

Lights are also characterized by the way they distribute light:

a) *Flood (or Broad).* Projects a wide angle beam from a scoop-shaped (diffusing) reflector rather than through a lens.

b) *Scoop.* A floodlight with a very wide beam.

c) *Spot.* Projects a precise, directional beam through a lens for controlled lighting and for highlighting subjects; uses a focusing reflector.

d) *Fresnel spot.* Identifiable by the stepped grooves on its lens; has an adjustable (narrow and wide) beam used for modeling and filling.

e) *Leko (ellipsoidal) light.* A projecting spot with a sharp-edged beam that can be focused into rectangular shapes used to highlight small areas over long distances. Because of its sharply defined beam, it is rarely used as a basic lighting instrument.

f) *Strip lights.* A series of flood lights along a strip providing general lighting.

g) *Specials.* Small spotlights with a narrow focus, used for highlighting.

h) *Inkies.* Small spotlights (lower wattage than specials) used to illuminate graphics.

i) *A Cucalorus (cuke),* similar to a stencil, inserted into a lekdite and used to produce patterns on a set or backdrop. *Barn doors* are flat pieces of metal, used like shades to adjust the parameters of a light's beam.

To achieve an effective balance, the back light should generally be the same intensity as the key light, but will vary depending upon the subject, background and desired effect (up to twice as strong as the key). If the back light is too intense, halos will result; if it is too low, it will be washed out. The usual ratio is 2:1—the side being half as strong as the primary light—but this ratio will also vary depending upon how bright or dark clothing, objects and the set are. To remove unnatural shadows, first try changing the existing lighting; additional lights may wash out the whole picture. Hot spots are probably being caused by a key light which is too bright: under less than ideal conditions, subjects can be placed against black backgrounds for more contrast.

Due to the nature of incandescent and quartz bulbs (the two basic sources of light),[4] never touch or allow moisture to come in contact with the surface—water or oil from the hands can cause the bulb to explode. Only handle lamps with electrician's gloves.

Shadowgrams

In addition to adding depth to a picture, shadows can be used in a completely abstract manner. Shadows can heighten or express elements of a setting, create a mood, provide a psychological backdrop or reflect the inner emotions of characters.[5]

A variety of effects can be achieved by placing an object or person between a light source and a wall. A large light will create a small, solid shadow; a small light, a larger shadow; and a pointed light, a sharp, hard-edged shadow. The closer the subject is to the light source, the larger the shadow. Wide-angle shadows exaggerate depth; uneven surfaces create distorted shadows; diffused, strong, weak, natural and grotesque shadows can be created by moving or changing the light source. The same techniques can be used to create silhouettes (placing a subject behind a translucent screen and projecting light onto the screen from the reverse side) or shadow plays.

Design a set using shadows rather than props. (How do you arrange the lights so that both shadows and actors may be seen? What compromises may be necessary?) Choose a selection from absurdist or avant-garde drama and use shadows to heighten elements of the scene; tape dramatic selections where low angle (bizarre) lighting and textures would be effective.

Sound

Soundwaves entering a microphone vibrate the diaphragm. Differences in frequency register as differences in pitch; the strength of the wave as volume. The audio head converts sound waves into magnetic signals and, just as a television tube reverses the photographic process during playback, an amplifier boosts the audio signal, sending it into a speaker which acts as a dynamic microphone in reverse.

The portapak has a microphone built into the camera, sufficient for initial explorations with the equipment or when operating alone, but limiting thereafter. External microphones (plugged into the deck's microphone jack) provide for more flexibility by increasing the distance between camera, microphone and subject, and can be placed on a table, floor stand, boom or attached to a person. Two types of microphones are generally used with the VTR: condensors (which are fragile, sensitive to sound, have a wide frequency range and reduce interference) and dynamic microphones (less sensitive and expensive, but more rugged and useful for outdoor locations). Both types are available in a number of "pick-up" patterns (see Table 1-5). The pattern chosen should be appropriate to the production needs.

TABLE 1.5: Microphones

a) *Unidirectional.* Sound enters from one direction only, reducing side, rear and background noises and reverberation. Appropriate for one-to-one interviews or productions where all sound originates directly in front of the microphone. Useful for isolating voices when shooting outdoors.

b) *Bidirectional.* Picks up sounds in front of and behind the microphone. Useful for two people facing each other, with one microphone in between.

c) *Omnidirectional.* A microphone built into the camera; picks up sound in a 360° pattern. Useful for recording groups of people, a number of sounds within an area and ambient noise. However, unwanted and background sounds are picked up as well. Useful in a soundproofed room where noises outside the classroom will not be picked up.

d) *Cardioid.* Records in a heart-shaped pattern, combining the best qualities of both directional and omnidirectional microphones. Useful for panel discussions.

e) *Lavalier.* A small microphone attached to the speaker's clothing, permitting greater mobility and decreasing microphone visibility. Clothing muffles extraneous sounds, but warn the students not to muffle all sounds by crossing their arms over their chests.

Unless a dramatic production is being taped, the sight of a microphone on the television screen is generally acceptable. Test the audio before starting the camera; placing a microphone too close to the source will result in unnatural sound quality and loss of "presence" (ambient sound creating the illusion of depth). A microphone placed too far away may emphasize the wrong sounds and diminish the intensity of the desired sound. Adjust microphone positions to accommodate individual differences—a voice that is too loud or soft, a person who constantly touches or grabs for the microphone (creating unwanted percussive sounds or, even worse, a battle for possession), a person who tends to lean away from or toward the camera or talks into his beard. If a long cord is required (over twenty feet) low impedance equipment will be necessary; high impedance mixers become necessary when several microphones are used. When setting up, consider how close the microphones need to be, how much cable is necessary, how noisy the environment will be, the amount of echo or reverberation present (drapes or other sound-absorbing material can be used in a room which is too "live") and be certain that all parts of the sound system are of the same impedance in order to prevent distortion, buzzes and hums.

Since portable units do not have VU (volume unit) meters to visually register sound levels, always monitor the sound with headphones. Listening with headphones will reveal extraneous room noise, poor microphone placement, or a microphone plug which has been pulled out. (This can be prevented by tying the cable around the deck's handle.) The VTR will automatically adjust for loud and soft sounds through its AGC (Automatic Gain Control) function. This is another useful device for the single-person crew, but one with the annoying habits of flattening sounds, cutting off highs and producing swelling effects in its efforts to equalize all sounds entering the microphone. This leaves the sound technician with limited control over the recording. (Nonportable decks have a manual adjustment to override the AGC.)

When taping outdoors, a cardboard baffle or windscreen can provide portable sound-proofing and reduce environmental noise; indoors, a boom can be created by hanging a microphone from a broomstick out of the camera's vision. Sound can be erased independently from the video and new sound recorded by using the dubbing control. The entire track or short portions can be replaced, or several new sources mixed together (with mixing equipment) to produce a more elaborate track. (Be certain to lower the volume on the monitor to avoid feedback.) While it is possible to re-record material, it is not possible to add material to an existing soundtrack (overdub) without erasing the original, unless a mixer and two recorders are used.

Notes

1. Gene Youngblood, *Expanded Cinema* (New York: E.P. Dutton, 1970), pp. 283-284.
2. Observe how light entering a room at different times of the day affects your mood. How do artificial lighting arrangements control mood and create atmosphere? What effect does movie theater, kitchen or department store lighting have on you?
3. Even brightly lit white lettering against a black background can cause a burn. A minor burn (dark spot) can be erased by aiming the camera, out of focus, at a neutral background.
4. Quartz bulbs are smaller, more efficient and more useful for color television than incandescent bulbs. However, they wear out faster, produce more heat and the beam cannot be controlled as precisely.
5. Puppeteers who otherwise would not be able to see their efforts will be able to analyze their performances on tape. A screening of *The Cabinet of Caligari,* the most famous example of the German psychological horror film, should provoke some ideas along these lines.

2

Contrast and Definition...
Visual Video Techniques

A combination of good content and good composition will be still more effective than good content alone. Really bad composition ... can seriously interfere with the viewer's enjoyment, or even his comprehension, of what is on the screen.[1]

Edward Stasheff and Rudy Bretz

The basics of video composition teach students how to communicate through the most effective combination of mechanical and visual elements. The composition of a shot can help clarify and support story content, heighten the aesthetic quality of an image, stimulate interest by providing variety and dynamism, increase the emotional impact of a scene (planned or impromptu) and heighten our enjoyment of video tape as an expressive medium.

By varying lenses and subject/camera distance, the same content can appear to change within a series of shots—each shot differing in depth, relative size among subjects and foreground/background relationships. Ask students to take the lens off the camera and turn on the monitor. What do they see? What cannot be seen? Which subject (object or person) dominates the picture? Why is your attention attracted to it? From what angle do you see the subject? How would you describe the elements in the foreground in relationship to the entire picture? What is happening in the background? Which elements appear to be taller? Larger? Too small to be seen? Out of focus? Which elements overlap? Are parts not visible? How deep does the image appear to be? Zoom out or in to a different shot and answer the questions again. Move the camera and look at the same area from a different angle. What happens to natural perspective when you widen the lens angle and move the camera closer to the subject to maintain subject size?

Anything that confuses, bores or disappoints the viewer, whether visual or dramatic, will weaken the production. The field of view (amount visible), angle (direction from which the subject is viewed), camera or subject movement, and composition chosen can all be used to provide variety, clarity and drama within a shot and within a series of shots. These same techniques enable the director to go beyond merely recording an event into areas such as aesthetics, manipulation, and psychology.

Structured techniques improve communication skills and allow students to achieve what they set out to do (an important first step: exploration and play—see "Video Games," Chapter 5.) Rules become language; restrictions become the means for acquiring new skills, ideas, and solutions. By exploring these techniques, students of any grade or ability level will heighten their awareness of design and the quality of images and potential movement within the frame, and they will learn about staging, directing and photographing.

Camera Shots

Shots[2] are classified by the field of view (area visible within the frame), area of subject visible (where the subject is cut by the lower edge of the frame) and number of subjects visible. For example, a *full figure* or *full-length shot* would include the entire subject within the frame, a *one shot* would include only one subject, a *two shot* two subjects, a *waist* or *thigh shot* would begin from those parts of the anatomy, and a *head shot*, only the head.

The four basic fields of view are the *long-shot* (LS), *mid-shot* (MS), *close-up* (CU) and *extreme close-up* (ECU). Shots are the visual equivalents of grammatical punctuation. Cutting from one to another can establish directions, show actions occurring in the same place, unify actions occurring in different places, and create symbolic images (visual metaphors). A typical series of shots might include a:

- LS of cars going up the first roller coaster hill

- MS of the first car as it comes over the top, passengers with arms raised

- CU of a frightened face

- ECU of an open, screaming mouth or ECU of hands now clutching the bar of the car

- MS of car completing its descent

- LS of coaster approaching a new hill

This is a very traditional approach to directing a sequence. Students will find themselves able to communicate their unusual and offbeat ideas more effectively once they have learned the "tried and true" methods. Pantomiming a roller coaster ride is also an excellent theater improvisation and video game.

The shot is relative to the subject being taped (determined by location, action and emphasis). In an instructional lesson on using video equipment, a sequence might include a LS of the camera, VTR and monitor; a MS of the VTR alone; a CU of the tape path and an ECU of the pause button.

If the year has started and you are still waiting for the video equipment to arrive, taking instant pictures of one another is a useful way to introduce shots, the excitement and immediacy of television (instantaneous results) and the science of photography (images developing on photosensitive papers).

The following "cameraless" exercise will familiarize students with basic photographic viewpoints and heighten their awareness of the compositional possibilities within a single image. These exercises can be especially useful when the equipment is out being repaired!

"Cameraless" exercises

1. Using a single work of art (photograph, painting, illustration or print from a book or magazine), reduce the work to simple geometric forms by focusing on shapes of figures and objects, shapes caused by groupings of figures and objects, and linear or circular patterns that move the eye from one group or figure to another. Cut out triangles, circles, rectangles and squares of different sizes from a sheet of cardboard and, using the cardboard as a stencil, frame different elements of the artwork. Try to discover smaller units and details of images you may not have noticed before, and sections of the work that might fit naturally into the geometric frames. If possible, obtain several copies of the work (so that parts of the same image may appear in different frames), cut out the details you have discovered, reassemble into a collage, or combine them with images from other sources to create a photomontage.

2. Make a simple "viewfinder" by cutting out two L-shaped pieces of cardboard and overlapping them so that the center area can be adjusted to simulate various shots. Slide the pieces over one another to frame different areas of a photograph or art reproduction, observing the effect different frames have on the same compositional unit.

Very young students can reinforce measurement, ratio, visual and distance skills by cutting a rectangle matching the screen ratio of 3:4 (e.g., 1½" x 2") in the middle of a piece of heavy-weight paper such as bristol board. Have them measure the rectangle, center and cut out the opening. Close one eye and look through the opening at one area of the room first, from arm's length, then with a bent elbow and finally with the viewfinder close to the eye. Ask them to do a quick drawing of what they see at each point, and to label the drawings as the various shots. Some students may enjoy making a "camera" by folding and stapling down the four edges of the paper, gluing on a paper button and flashcube, doing the drawings on a very small pieces of paper, placing the papers inside the folded edge, looking through the viewfinder and producing instant "photographs." If children have difficulty making the transition from holding the viewfinder at arm's length to calling the result a close-up, move them physically closer and further away from objects in the room.

3. Use the viewfinder (by closing and opening the pieces of cardboard or moving the "camera" forward and back) to simulate a zoom, revealing more or less area content in a continuous movement.

4. Show a variety of pictures and photographs to demonstrate how artists and photographers frame their works in equivalent fields of view.

Composition

Framing

A frame limits our point of view; it establishes order where it did not exist, and creates disorder by changing relationships.

To help define the possibilities and limitations of the frame, keep the camera stationary and ask a subject to fill the entire screen with his or her face. Ask the subject to fill the screen with different body parts, and finally to fit his entire body into the frame. Fit several bodies into the frame.

Keeping the subject stationary, use the camera (by changing the lens or physically moving the camera) to fill the screen with the subject's face, different body parts and several subjects.

Keeping the camera stationary, ask the subject to enter and, while watching himself in the monitor, to touch the bottom of the frame, the top and either side of the frame. By moving the camera instead of the subject, have the subject appear to touch various parts of the frame, to put his feet on the ceiling, and elbows on the bottom of the screen.[3]

The choice of shot and subject's position within the frame can be used to achieve specific dramatic effects. Focus on one person. How does a LS affect the subject's relationship to the set or background? What effect does a CU of the same subject have? When would you use an ECU? How close can a subject get to the camera without becoming a blur? How far away without losing facial detail? Frame the same subject in different ways to achieve a variety of psychological, visual, and dramatic effects. What shot or sequence of shots (of the same subject) would students choose to communicate alienation? Fear? Stability?

In live broadcasting or "on the spot" taping, a loose frame or shot (i.e., one in which the subject or subjects are surrounded by areas of space separating them from the frame) is valuable since it can accommodate large and unexpected actions. When a documentary is being shot, it can help the cameraperson locate and isolate important details within a larger framework. In a scripted production, a tighter frame with less surrounding space (the subject crowds the sides of the frame) is generally preferable. A shot which is too loose wastes space, introduces distracting background elements and results in poor composition. A shot which is too tight can appear cramped, may amputate (crop) parts of the subject, leave out important elements of the scene and may not leave enough room for sudden large movements.

Frame two subjects so that there is enough space to avoid crowding but not so much that they are lost in space. Tape and play back two players at an athletic event (e.g., tennis). Was any action lost outside the frame? Were subjects too small to be seen? Frame a single person (in a CU) so that sufficient headroom is left between the top of the frame. (Too much space is as bad as too little.)

POOR COMPOSITION: too much space between camera and subject. The picture can be improved by altering the angle of the shot or the camera/subject placement.

ANOTHER EXAMPLE of poor composition. The center of interest is hard to find against the background, and the picture as a whole lacks dominance.

Balance

A balanced picture does not necessarily mean a symmetrical one. While a single person may be centered an equal distance from the sides of the frame, the subject's head would not be positioned equally distant from the top and bottom of the frame. The picture would be poorly balanced and have too much space on top. When a print is matted, it is usually framed with more space on the bottom and less on top.

Avoid placing identical forms in two halves of the frame, and placing subjects along horizontal or vertical lines which divide the picture in half. A perfectly symmetrical picture is confusing (the viewer does not know which half to look at), lacks dominance, calls attention to the frame rather than the picture, and is uninteresting. Off-center framing also has the advantage of including elements within the frame that would not appear in a symmetrical one. Balance is also affected by tone. Heavier (darker) tones imply mass and can be used to balance larger lighter tones, create an oppressive feeling (placed at the top of the picture), or sense of stability (placed at the bottom).

Balancing the composition: exercises

1. Ask subjects to stand randomly in front of the camera. Simplify and organize the picture by creating different groups (moving the camera and/or the subjects).

2. Ask three people to stand apart from one another. Try moving subjects closer together to form two groups (one plus two), and create different groupings by working in depth so that forms overlap.

3. Form larger groups into specific shapes (triangles, circles and squares in two dimensions; cubes, spheres and pyramids in three dimensions; T-shapes, crosses and X-shapes) to achieve a balanced picture.

4. Try to achieve balance when working with levels; arrange groups on furniture or props of different heights.

5. Demonstrate stability (the subject is securely positioned), instability (the subject is positioned along diagonal lines), and neutrality (the subject could be ready for motion) with the same person.

Balance is affected not only by what is inside the frame, but by what is occurring outside the frame. Space (lead room) needs to be left in the frame for a person talking with the subject from off-screen, for something or someone about to enter the frame, or for something the subject is headed toward (anticipating the flow of movement—see "Camera Movement," page 34) unless a special effect is desired such as having the subject pressed against one side of the frame to express frustration, helplessness, or extreme fear, or if an action is taking place behind the subject. Direct a subject to talk with another person off-screen to the left, and frame the subject in a close-up. Where should the subject appear to achieve the best balance?

Other considerations

Avoid high contrast images (the camera has a limited contrast ratio); high contrasts with skin tones or in clothing; finely detailed patterns (thin stripes, checks, herringbone) which interfere with the scanning lines and distract the viewer; and highly reflective jewelry that disrupts the picture's balance. Students can tape what they happen to be wearing at the moment to demonstrate possible problems.

Emphasis

A close-up is the easiest (and most obvious) way to emphasize a subject. Variations in size, height, shape and angle are other ways of achieving interest and dominance within a frame. If all the subjects on the screen are the same size, the result is generally uninteresting. Difference in size creates variety and focuses our attention on elements within the frame.

Exercises illustrating emphasis

Without moving the camera or changing lenses, direct a small group of students so that each member of the group appears to be the same size (i.e., equally important), then re-direct the group in both two and three dimensions to emphasize different individuals. A subject standing downstage (closer to the audience) will be larger and dominate the screen as long as he or she faces the audience. What occurs if a person downstage faces *away* from the audience?

Change lenses or physically move the camera, rather than regroup the subjects, to achieve variety in size. Try photographing the group at an angle rather than head on.

A low angle shot can be achieved by raising the subject or lowering the camera; a high angle shot (above the eye-level of the subject) by raising the camera or lowering the subject; and an overhead shot by shooting straight down at the floor. While you may not want to literally suspend yourself from the rafters, the portapak does have an advantage over studio equipment; it enables you to shoot from a variety of angles difficult to obtain or impractical to set up in a studio.

Photograph the same subject from above and below. Photograph a group of subjects from below (near subjects will appear higher) and above eye level (subjects in the rear will lengthen). Diminish or exaggerate the natural size or height of individuals. Have one subject appear to dominate another. A person higher in the frame tends to dominate one lower. (When might the opposite be true? Explore the dramatic possibilities of "looking up to" or "down at" a subject.)

Use triangular shapes to achieve emphasis. A triangular space in the center of the screen leaves two triangular shapes on either side. Try placing the subject in all three triangles respectively to discover which triangle is of the greatest importance. The top angle of a triangle is in the dominant position. What happens to the center of interest in an inverted triangular arrangement? Stage a variety of shots to achieve an organized composition and emphasize the

SHOOTING FROM DIFFERENT angles or directions changes the emphasis of a scene. Above, a high angle shot of a video interview; below, the camera has moved 180 degrees around the subjects for a reverse shot of the same scene.

center of interest. Evaluate by determining to which part of the screen the viewer's eye is immediately drawn.

Unless a particularly surrealistic or disorienting effect is desired, always find a natural motivation for the grouping—some subjects standing, some seated on arms of chairs as they would be in real situations. Use techniques such as differences in height, size, lighting, differentiation of movement, placement of the subject at the apex of a triangle, and converging lines of force (see below) to achieve the best composition and to express dominance.

Use size to emphasize dominance in a dramatic relationship. Set up an over-the-shoulder shot and use vertical movement (the tilt) to shift emphasis from one stationary figure to another. Write a brief scene around a relationship where the roles become reversed (the dominant person becomes submissive, and the submissive takes control). Do not state the exchange directly in the dialogue, but communicate it visually.

Line

Subjects placed along horizontal or vertical lines give the impression of stability; diagonal lines show movement (a principle exploited by the Russian filmmakers and Futurist artists of the 1920s). Curved lines create feelings of movement, change, and grace. (Upward curves imply openness; downward curves, restriction.)

"Line" exercises

Arrange subjects along diagonal lines for passive/active emphasis.

Stage a scene where all players are looking in different directions (lines of sight do not converge), where all are looking at one focal point, and where all are looking in the same direction—except for one. Apply the same principles to emphasize movement or stasis; all subjects move in the same direction, all move quickly or slowly except for the "center of attention," or all move down while one moves up.

Apply design principles to clothing considerations. Vertical lines emphasize height and narrow proportions; horizontal, width and bulk.

Lighting

As already stated, light not only makes an image possible but contributes to the quality of that image. You can improve the composition of a shot by reducing the light in distracting elements and highlighting important ones or achieve dominance by focusing light on the subject. Use backlighting to separate the subject from the background (especially useful when taping dancers). Perhaps you could write a scene where areas of light are added one at a time to reveal something new about the composition, resulting in a cumulative effect.

Backgrounds and sets

The background (whether natural or a set) and the subject's relationship to the background are integral parts of the composition.

Frame the background in a variety of ways to achieve the best composition. You may design a background or set so that individual areas will create interesting compositions. Consider what the clothing, costumes (if any), objects, lighting, and movement will look like against it. The same principles concerning placement along horizontal and vertical lines with the frame apply to backgrounds as well. (A simple background is especially important when taping dancers, for example, or physical education classes, since the figures will be small and movement must be clearly differentiated from the background). Be certain props work to your advantage.

Perspective and depth

Television has not yet been blessed with stereoscopic (3-D) vision or holographic pictures. However, perspective and depth can be used to advantage on a two-dimensional surface.

You can heighten the illusion of space on the screen by using techniques such as placing objects downstage to exaggerate a foreground/background distance, and using wide-angle lenses. In the theater, proper perspective can be seen by only a few members of the audience since they are seated at different angles from the stage. The television picture is not (currently) three-dimensional, and all viewers can observe the scene in perspective if the foreground and background perspectives have been properly matched. To achieve this, the horizon line should be drawn at camera level—the horizon of the picture should coincide with the real horizon.

Camera role

When the first one-minute films were presented during the mid-1890s, the camera merely served as a recording device. The field of view remained the same. The set was moved closer to the camera rather than the camera moved into the set. Now, both television and movie cameras serve a variety of functions, from completely objective to completely subjective, and often combine functions within a single production.

Camera Movement

The pan

A pan is created by pivoting the camera in a lateral direction from a fixed position, and is used to follow horizontal action, lead the viewer over a wide area or static scene, or reveal new elements within an area.[4] When a stationary camera records a moving subject, the subject appears to be moving against a stationary background. When a camera moves along with the subject (keeping the framing constant), the subject appears to be motionless against a background that is moving in the opposite direction. A pan must be continuously interesting with a motivated beginning, visually interesting middle, and specific conclusion (goal).

Ask one student to walk from right to left in front of the camera, then left to right while the camera follows his or her movement. Observe the pan on playback. Did the pan start and stop smoothly (the camera should be held steady just before starting and after ending the pan)? Was the movement slow, level, continuous and flowing? Did the camera lag behind or stay with the subject by anticipating the subject's motion?

Ask the subject to move in discontinuous patterns (back and forth, slowly and quickly) while the cameraperson tries to follow smoothly. Try following the action in a basketball game, skateboard contest, or swimming meet.

Pan across a relatively stationary setting or scene, such as a skyline or landscape, to emphasize the expanse or relationship among parts. How quickly does the camera need to move? How would the speed of the pan differ between scenes with relatively little action or detail and those with more movement or detail?

Create and tape a situation that dictates the use of a "whiz" (panning so quickly that everything is a blur).

Find or write examples of scenes where a pan can be used to explore the set and reveal things one at a time, or where the discovery of objects builds to a cumulative effect.

For on-the-spot shooting, use the pan to seek out areas of interest or provide variety if there is no action to follow. (Use any natural movement such as people moving or following paths along buildings in one direction at a time.)

The tilt

Similar to the pan, the tilt can be used as a bridge, for creating high or long angle shots, for following the action of someone rising from a seated position, revealing something previously not visible within the frame, or following vertical action.

The dolly

Dollying involves the physical movement of the camera closer to or farther away from the subject. (The camera shoots while it is moving). The motivation for a dolly (like any camera movement) is to show the audience what it wants to see at a given moment or to stimulate interest as it moves in to a CU. Watch for dollies on television, and identify what *you* wanted to see that motivated the movement. How often does the camera dolly in a situation comedy? In an action program? Look for examples where rapid dollying is used for dramatic emphasis or to achieve a strong kinesthetic effect; observe how dollies are used at the beginnings and ends of some programs, in the middle for variety, and for general composition.

Fluidity and continuity are as important when dollying as when panning or tilting. Experiment with the effects different focal lengths have on fluidity of movement—the shorter the lens (wider the angle) the smoother the action, since a long lens emphasizes erratic camera movement. This is especially useful when dollying on a rough surface or from a less-than-sturdy vehicle.[5]

Focus on a stationary subject (a person standing in a doorway, against a bulletin board . . . anything other than a blank wall). Dolly in to a MS from a LS; return to the LS and move in to a MS using the zoom lens. Observe the different effect each technique has on the figure and on the figure/ground relationship. With a dolly the viewer is moved past foreground objects, changing the perspective without changing the angle of vision. The image becomes deeper, and the distance between objects becomes exaggerated as near objects move in relationship to far objects. During a zoom the viewer's physical relationship with the objects remains unaltered, but the angle of vision is narrowed to exclude foreground objects. The distance between objects is compressed, the image does not deepen, and the perspective remains the same (an object obscured at the widest angle will remain obscured at the narrowest). When would you choose to zoom, and when to dolly? Try combining the zoom and dolly.

The truck and arc

The truck is used to follow a subject's lateral movement by moving the camera, with its mount, parallel to the subject. The arc is a combination truck, dolly and pan. Some examples are listed below.

1. Follow a subject's movement to the left or right by moving the camera along with the subject (trucking). Observe how elements in the foreground move more quickly than those in the background, increasing the feeling of depth.

2. Focusing on a stationary subject, move the camera to either side in curved paths (arcs). The camera will need to pan in the opposite direction of the arc in order to maintain the subject and size of the shot while the angle changes.

3. Experiment with diagonal and curved paths in combination with a moving subject. When might a particularly fluid camera movement be appropriate?

Other shots

Establishing shot

Generally a LS establishes the scene and includes such information as where the scene is taking place and who or what will be involved in the action. The viewer should have no difficulty in locating himself; two shots might be necessary if both an exterior and interior are being used.

A disorienting start ("Where am I?") can be useful in some productions, but if the viewer is kept guessing too long he may become frustrated and lose interest in what follows. Find examples of "establishing shots" in literature including verbal equivalents of long, mid and close-up shots. Compare the orderly or nonorderly use of "shots" in literature to their use or nonuse in poetry. Try creating a tape which completely disorients the viewer—one photographed in such a manner that a familiar place becomes forbidding, unidentifiable or abstract.

Cover shot

A LS covers the total activity included within a large area so the viewer can follow several subjects or parts of the action at once.

Re-establishing shot

A MS or LS is used to remind the audience where it is, to introduce new elements into the scene or to relocate the viewer (serving as a transition to the next scene). A brief interview might begin with a LS to set the scene, follow with a MS of the subject and interviewer, CU of the subject, reaction shot of the interviewer (see below), and MS of the two people to re-establish the general scene. The re-establishing shot can be accomplished by zooming or dollying back, panning after pulling back, or using a reverse angle shot, and can also be used to help clarify two scenes taking place in two different places. ("Meanwhile, back at the ranch....")

Reaction shot

Someone says something, someone responds. The will is read, and the camera cuts to a series of responses (a horrified face, delighted face, shrugged shoulder, fainting lady). The statement or action is the motivation; the success of the shot depends upon timing (when you cut) and method (how you cut). Avoid parades of posed reactions.[6]

Over-the-shoulder shot

The camera is placed behind and looks over the shoulder of one subject at the second subject, enabling both subjects to remain in view. The dominant subject (facing the audience) may be reacting to what the first subject is saying, or leading the conversation.

Reverse angle shot

The first shot shows the action from one direction; the second, from the opposite direction. (The camera is turned a full 180 degrees but stays on the same side of the line of action.) The reverse angle shot is also used to re-establish the scene.

Framed shot

This is created by framing a subject with parts of an object or person—e.g., framing one person through the arms or legs of another, shooting from under a table (framing with the legs and underside of the table), or through a wire fence. A framed shot, like any unusual shot, should not be overused. Within a traditional dramatic structure it needs to be motivated, resolved and led away from to be incorporated smoothly. Even in a surrealistic tape, using framed shots just to be unusual will only succeed in looking superficial and "arty."

Odd juxtaposition

Two unrelated objects or people appear to be related, the association resulting in a third image: a woman with a tail (a dog trailing behind the woman), a man with the head of a statue (a man, seen from behind, lowers his head to fix his tie and the head of the statue appears to be on the man's shoulders). This is generally considered to be a poorly composed shot (incorrect choice of camera angle), but for a satiric production or visual comment on an aspect of a character's personality, the shot could be used to advantage.

Mattes

Different framing effects can be created by cutting out a shape from the bottom of a paper cup, painting the inside black, and attaching the cup to the lens. The entire bottom of the cup can be removed, clear acetate attached and vaseline rubbed around the edges to create a romantic, partially out-of-focus effect. A matte consisting of a scenic foreground not fastened to the camera is called a "gobo," and can be mounted on an easel or a stand.

Glass shot

This is similar to a gobo, but produces a cumulative effect. A scene painted on glass (usually leaving the center area open) is mounted between the camera and background. The camera shoots through the glass, resulting in a composite image of live subjects and painted scenery.

Canted shot

For special dramatic effects, the subject appears to tilt toward one of the upper corners of the frame. Since the camera cannot be used for any other shot without remounting the entire camera, the canted shot is impractical to set up in a professional studio but is easily accomplished with a portapak by shortening one leg of the tripod and shooting sideways. Vertical and horizontal lines no longer appear as they should; strong diagonal lines dominate.

The same canted effect can be achieved by attaching a dove prism or by placing a mirror to the side of the subject with its surface angled off the vertical plane.

Mirrors

The range of special effects available to users of the portapak is limited without additional equipment. However, as the list below shows, a variety of illusions can be created by simple arrangements of mirrors.

1. High angle shot. Instead of hanging the camera overhead, a similar effect can be achieved by shooting into a mirror reflecting the action from above (right and left will be reversed).

2. Reflections. Place a small mirror parallel and as close to the center of the camera lens as possible. (Increase the light if the image is too dark.) This creates the illusion of a reflection.

3. Split-screen. Set a large mirror at a 45-degree angle to the camera, extending half way across the frame. The split-screen effect is created by viewing half of the image directly, the other half reflected. A soft or hard edge down the center of the screen can be achieved by moving the mirror closer to the lens or closer to the subject.

4. Superimposition. Two images can be made to appear at once by shooting through an angled sheet of plate glass mounted on a floor stand. The camera sees the actual scene occurring behind the glass and the image reflected by the glass.[7]

Notes

1. Edward Stasheff and Rudy Bretz, *The Television Program* (New York: Hill and Wang, 1951), pp. 99-100.

2. A "shot" is a given composition—any uninterrupted length of taped or filmed action occurring in the same time and place. When the camera stops ("cuts") to change positions, lenses or locations, a new shot begins. Dramatically, a series of shots becomes a scene; a group of scenes comprises a sequence.

3. The three exercises above are adapted from Quincy Bent's "Introductory Video Exercises" in *Video and Kids (Radical Software,* Vol. 2, no. 6).

4. For studio work, use a friction-head tripod. For hand-held shooting, stand with a solid base, weight forward, with feet pointed in the direction in which the pan will end. Use the elbow of one arm against the stomach as a brace, the other hand to brace the camera when not focusing or zooming, and pan by swiveling the entire body from the waist up in one smooth motion.

5. The tripod can be attached to a light weight collapsible dolly or the cameraperson can be wheeled along in a wheelchair.

6. A smooth transition can be accomplished by overlapping the voice just preceding the reaction onto the reaction. To do this with the portapak, the overlapping words would need to be dubbed in later. Since lip synchronization is not needed, the transition can be effected by stopping the words at a natural place just before the cut and then continuing after the cut.

7. Techniques for creating wipes and other effects by using mirrors can be found in Rudy Bretz, *Techniques of Television Production* (New York: McGraw-Hill, 2nd ed., 1962), and Gerald Millerson, *The Technique of Television Production* (New York: Hastings House, 9th ed., 1972).

3

Prime Time Dramatization. . . From Story Idea to Treatment

A single idea, in writing as in the visual arts, can be developed in a seemingly infinite number of ways.[1]

Anthony Garcia and Robert Myers

When we talk about a "good" production, we are talking about program content and the learning derived from the production process, not about professional-looking results that are impossible with portable half-inch video tape equipment.[2]

John LeBaron and Louise Kanne

Children who avoid live dramatic presentations often become willing participants in video productions. Those who are convinced they will fail can make mistakes and correct themselves without feeling humiliated in front of an audience of peers. Dramatization heightens students' contact with themselves and their world, and enables them to start from where they feel most comfortable ... their own experiences, the personalities and experiences of others, even unrealities (masks and puppets). Dramatic situations are everywhere—in human behavior, random bits of dialogue, one's own daily life.

Screenplays

The effectiveness of a screenplay is not based upon how well it reads (as is a novel), but on how effective it is describing scenes to be photographed, dialogue to be heard and actions to be seen.[3] A movie script, utilizing the advantages of that medium, could not be produced directly on television. A home audience is not a captive one and television is not viewed in the company of a large audience. A "dead spot" in the dialogue, deliberately timed after a laugh in film, would be inappropriate after a scripted laugh in television. (There would be no audience reaction to drown out the dialogue.) Without an audience full of people to show one another

41

how to react, television producers often have to supply the cues (e.g., canned laughter, or the chuckling plunkets—see Appendix B, "Stay Tuned: Listening Skills").

A play produced for theatrical presentation cannot be used, unaltered, as a screenplay. Perform a live drama, then videotape it. How is it different for the audience? What audience responses present during the live production are now missing? What is the psychological impact of television techniques such as the reaction shot, or the ability of a subject to look directly into the camera?

Story ideas

Extraordinary ideas are found in the most ordinary places—ourselves, the environment and the ways in which we interact with that environment. Dramatic and comic situations can be developed through improvisation, still photography, watching television ... any activity that involves students in looking, listening and feeling.

Improvisation as a resource

Fantasy is a natural part of child development, and acting out stories is a natural part of videotaping. Improvised situations can be developed into themes and plays by outlining the action on the blackboard during playback, further setting the action during a second recording, and finalizing the action with appropriate camera cues and direction during a third recording.

Clichés. Write situations around, and act out, dialogue clichés. Then develop less archaic ways of communicating the same ideas.[4] (A list of clichés is given below.)

TABLE 3.1:Clichés for Dialogue Development

- "Don't worry, everything is going to be all right."
- "You mean...." (Fearfully asked, preceding the horrible or startling revelation.)
- "But my son was always such a good boy." (Spoken by the grieving mother of a homicidal maniac.)
- "Why, you look as if you've seen a ghost!"
- "That's *our* song they're playing."
- "No, don't look back. I want to remember you like this."
- "Hold me close, darling! Closer! Closer! Don't ever let me go!"
- "There's only one man who can save him...." (And he's on vacation in the Himalayas.)
- "Follow that car!"
- "Stop the presses!"
- "I'm comin' out and I'm comin' out shooting !"
- "We're through, washed up, finished—you hear me!"
- "Yes, I killed him! Sure I did! and I'm glad! You hear me—I'm glad!"
- "Pull yourself together!" (Often accompanied by a slap and a "I needed that.")

Justifications. Improvise shapes with your body. At a given signal, freeze and justify (think about) your position in terms of *what* you might be doing—looking for a contact lens, scratching your back, or rowing a boat; create new shapes and freeze again, justifying the position as an animal or person (*who* you are—a traffic officer, street cleaner, teacher, dog); create shapes a third time and justify *where* you are (a location).

Who am I? One student comes up in front of the class and tries to demonstrate, nonverbally, who he or she is through body position, movement, posture and physical activity. This is used for building characters and identifying nonverbal actions that distinguish characters.

Other improvisations. Act out short stories, literary expressions used by authors, selections from the classic oral narratives, folk tales, poems, proverbs and fables. Read, then experience scenes from classic plays by acting them out, and finally write a new screenplay in the style of the one studied.

Begin performing literary selections, but at some point alter the story. Provide a new ending for an old story. Choose a theme (e.g. courage), read selections from several literary sources concerning that theme, discuss the various treatments, and improvise a scene using one of the treatments as a basis. Prepare scenes by placing characters in different situations, exploring how they would react under different conditions (physical or emotional) or when confronted by another character, or when given a different motivation.

Carry a notebook and write down bits of overheard conversations. Using the fragments, develop dramatic situations concerning the actions of real people.

Still photography as a resource

Shoot photographs of things that interest you, based on what you already know about them; shoot photographs of events, actions, places and things as you newly experience or discover them. Look at someone else's photograph one day; on the next day try to recall as many details about the photograph as possible, then confirm your recollections. What helped you to remember certain items? Did personal associations enable you to recall details?

"Read" a photograph. Analyze it by identifying the subject (noun), action (verb), context (setting) and relationship to the viewer (shot). Analyze the photographer's attitude toward his or her subject in terms of lighting, point of view, framing and clarity of image. Identify and label objects, sort out and describe supportive details (adjectives and adverbs), infer probable or actual facts, and interpret relationships. Write stories based on the photographs, including what led up to and what will follow the given action.

Characterization

The central characters in a drama must be three-dimensional (unless the production is deliberately cartoon-like), credible and able to elicit empathy from the audience. Characterization and plot are interconnected; the characters' personalities and motivation are portrayed through their reactions to various situations, particularly those involving conflict. (See discussion of plot later in this chapter.)

What the audience sees is usually only a fraction of a person's life: The character (even the sets) must convey a strong sense of "before" and "after," an existence that has evolved to this point in time and will continue to develop after the screen goes blank.

Minor characters should be developed with the same care as major ones—they add contrast, create subplots and, in a television series, provide continuity and conflict. The most successful series use the star as a stabilizing force rather than the constant center of interest; the star is drawn *into* the minor character's actions and does not always *cause* the conflict. The episode becomes less dependent upon the star personality and relies more on the supporting players acting in an ensemble manner. The stronger the minor characters, the greater the plot possibilities. (See Table 3.5.)

Visual elements can also be used to support characterizations, but should not be distracting. Props can be used to help identify and develop characters, to develop suspense, to improve composition—or simply to provide nervous actors with something to do.

Script formats

The most common format for a script uses a paper divided lengthwise in half. The left-hand column is headed VIDEO and contains information such as the sequence of shots, transitions, visuals, composition of each shot, and all information for the director and cameraman. The right-hand column is headed AUDIO and includes dialogue, narration, music, sound effects (everything from simple cue sentences to a full script). Where substantial camera movement is required, tape separate "shot sheets" onto the camera(s) listing lens, type of shot and camera movement.

Scripts contain as much information as necessary for the particular production. A panel discussion or interview program would need very few directions since it is ad-libbed; a half-hour drama, on the other hand, would need to indicate every direction for the production to run smoothly. Three-column scripts add a storyboard to the audio and visual columns; four-column formats further divide audio into sound effects or music, and dialogue or narration. Other variations include a two-column script using a storyboard on one side, the script on the other; a three-column narration, script, shot and storyboard combination (for instructional television); and four-column shot, content and arrangement of scene, dialogue or narration, and music or sound effects. Professional screenplays follow a slightly different format indicating "interior" or "exterior," place and time on one line; transitions on the next (e.g., "fade in"); a description of the type of shot, subject and action; the character's name; descriptive guides for reading the lines (e.g., "terrified"); and finally the actual dialogue—all typed down the center of the page. See Table 10.1 for a sample script of a commercial.

Program formats

Watch and compare different program formats. For example, which programs occur at what times during the day? Where and how long are the commercial interruptions in a news program or dramatic presentation? When and where do noncommercial interruptions appear, and how long are they? How much general patter is there in a variety show? A talk program? How much time is allotted to the star? How would you feel if your favorite series suddenly changed its format or time slot? Which programs are live, taped and on film? What would be the effect if the program was transmitted through a different medium (tape rather than film)?

A series format is constructed in a particular manner to provide continuity from week to week. Improvise and tape common scenes from several formats—a soap opera, western, family sit-com, detective or police story, medical program. What dialogue, characters, and situations are invariably used? Refer back to the television set. How close did the improvisation come to the actual format?

Achieving Visual Continuity

The writer has already seen the action in his mind; the director now needs to visualize the story on paper before it goes into production. The effectiveness of a visual story (whether on film or television) is determined by its continuity. Communicating through moving images in both narrative and non-narrative forms requires an understanding of design and composition within the frame and an awareness of flow from frame to frame. An understanding of visual continuity is essential to any visual medium to organize time and space in linear and nonlinear sequences, to communicate messages clearly and dramatically, to develop visual literacy and to use production elements most effectively. Sequencing is a fundamental educational process that helps students build skills in arranging isolated parts into a meaningful order, recognizing groups of related images and actions, and using those designs as a form of creative expression.

Design sequences: using content to move from one shot to another

Collect visual images from magazines and newspapers and arrange them in groups according to common characteristics or qualities such as shape, line, overall design, balance, space, color, texture, lighting and distance. Create continuity boards by exploring the composition within each picture and by arranging the pictures in sequence according to the following methods.

Serialization

Each image has something in common with the one immediately preceding and following it, but not necessarily with any other image in the sequence. (A sequence of eight images is convenient to start.)

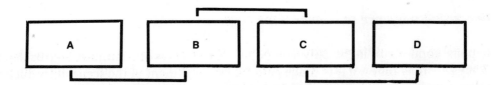

'A' relates to 'B' through a common quality; 'B' to 'C' through another common quality; 'C' to 'D' and so on. There is, however, no direct link between 'A' and 'D.'

Sets

Build a set of three or four images based on a single quality, then find something in the last image of the set to serve as a link to a new set of three or four. Continue until at least four sets have been arranged.

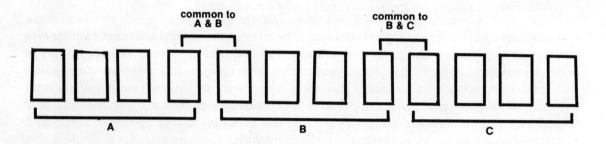

Varying patterns

Use the same approach as above, but shift the number of images within the sets to create a sense of visual rhythm and emphasis.

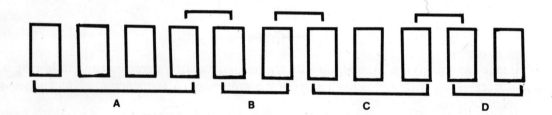

Although the viewer may not think in terms of 4-2-3-2, the eye will perceive something of this effect. Try varieties of combinations to achieve different rhythms.

Storyline: using sequence to convey a message

Four-panel comic strips in the daily newspaper are examples of continuity boards that tell a story. They generally follow a four-stage pattern: establishment of the scene, introduction of the conflict, development of the conflict and conflict resolution. The four-frame structure, in dramatic terms, consists of the *condition* of the action, *cause* of the action, resulting action or *climax* and answer to the climax—*resolution*.

Analyze comic strips for their sequencing techniques. Observe the visual elements used to convey the storyline, the ways individual frames or shots function (i.e., the compositional elements within them) and how the frames are sequenced (the linkage between the elements).

Storyboarding: the application of visual continuity

Storyboarding is the director's attempt to visually detail the action and shot to be used at each stage of a story, and is a more practical approach to changing material than editing and reshooting video tape. Though usually associated with television and film, storyboards date back to the earliest recorded messages. Pictorial sequences of events and myths are found, for example, in cave paintings, Egyptian tombs and Greek friezes.

Sequences can be thematic or narrative in nature. A thematic board takes a particular idea and develops a visual expression of it. This can be analytical (showing various aspects or facets) or relational (showing how the idea touches other ideas, events, phenomena) and may not have a clear beginning, middle and end. A narrative board tells a story in a linear manner—how an event or a series of actions came about, or how a movement occurred logically in time and space.

Always start with more images than you intend to use. Photographs or art work can be mounted and arranged four to a page, sequenced on long strips or displayed "accordian" style. (Most continuity boards can subsequently serve as the basis for a video tape.)

Thematic boards

Ask students to maintain a record of their dreams over a period of time. Find pictures that relate to or directly visualize the dream, then sequence the images. Since events in dreams may not occur logically in time and space, images should be connected through design rather than storytelling principles. (Dream boards provide a useful transition from design sequences to narrative boards since they combine elements of both.)

Choose a documentary subject and proceed as above. Images can be related in a linear-narrative style, or through design principles.

Narrative boards

Here you need a still camera, one photographer and one or more actors. Choose an activity that develops logically in time and space—an event with a built-in direction (building or destroying something) or an activity with a clear product (painting a mural) or result. The photographer works independently from the actors, photographing but not interfering with the action. Choose several of the resulting photographs and create a dramatic storyboard that still conveys a sense of the action as it actually occurred.

Or you can use a chase as a subject, establish the scene, create a conflict, develop the action (the chase), and resolve it. Proceed as above. The finished board should convey a sense of the action dramatically and logically as it occurred in time as well as space. Try using two photographers for a variety of angles and viewpoints. If photographs are pasted on index cards, sequences can be shuffled and given to other students, who attempt to resequence them in the intended order.

Visual Treatment

Multiple cameras, switchers, mixers, effects generators and editing decks are not indispensable to manipulating images. The single system is extremely flexible and, with planning, can provide professional results. If you are fortunate enough to have an elaborate studio don't ignore the single system as being too simplistic. Developing the maximum potential of one camera/one deck will teach students skills it might take quite a bit longer to unravel beneath all the fancy equipment.

Blocking action

The director provides unity, pacing, continuity, and artistic viewpoint and blocks out (sets up) the action on a floor plan prior to taping. The most important aspect of blocking for the single-system production is to provide maximum continuity with minimum camera movement. Potential problems that follow focus, radical or cumbersome shot changes, obscured or poorly lit subjects or visuals, and poor camera movement can be controlled by walking through the production and identifying the position of the talent and order of the visual materials presented to establish camera positions. The placement of talent and order of visuals should be known to the cameraperson if the production is fully scripted, and is essential for improvised shooting. Knowledge of how action is likely to proceed leads to more effective productions in the classroom and on location.

Not all productions follow a storyboard or are completely blocked. Interviews, panel and small group discussions (moderated or unmoderated), "talk programs," news events and many documentaries do not follow a script. The choice of shot and development of continuity is left to the cameraperson. The techniques below (Table 3.2) will be useful for creating pacing and variety with one camera during unscripted shooting.

TABLE 3.2: Camera Techniques for Pacing and Variety

- *Move the camera.* Vary the speed, moving from one subject to another. Cut to capture action (opening the view to include all the action), or capture a reaction.

- *Zoom.* Vary the speed of the zoom. Zoom in for intensity, out as the conversation relaxes. Keep a loose mid-shot generally.

- *Use natural motivation.* Anticipate movement by looking for nonverbal reactions, listening for transitional pauses (ends of phrases or thoughts), pacing, and direction of the conversation.

- *Move the camera from one speaker to another.* Open to a two-or-three-person shot from one person speaking, zoom out at moderate speed to a cover shot when the speaker is finished, and go on to the next speaker (a V formation is best for three or more subjects).

- *If there is no action ...* Maintain a tight close-up of whatever action there is; shoot reactions; zoom out to locate action; look for contrasts.

- *When shooting crowds and demonstrations ...* look for large patterns (swaying and group movement) and small motions.

The same concerns about composition within a frame apply to movement from one frame to another. It must be motivated and natural. To observe the amount of flexibility available even within these guidelines, ask three independent groups to block the same section of a script and compare the results.

Enlarging action

Events happening in reality are often too brief for us to become completely involved, or to sustain our interest. It is usually necessary to manipulate events in real time to keep an audience involved in actions occurring on the screen. Given here are two different ways to deal with action.

> *Action:* Two teams of students having a tug of war.
> *Treatment #1*

> (LS) Teams gather at either end of a mud hole, lift the rope and begin pulling.
> (MS) Team members closest to the mud hole are pulling in opposite directions.
> (LS) Zoom out as one team is pulled into the mud.

> *Treatment #2*

> (LS) Teams gather at either side of a mud hole.
> (MS) Zoom in as opposing team members closest to mud hole taunt each other.
> (CU) Zoom in to rope being pulled taut.
>   Pan expressions on faces of one team, then the other team as the contest goes on.
> (MS) Pained expressions on faces of several members of Team 'A.'
> (MS) Triumphant expressions on faces of several members of opposing team 'B.'
> (MS) Triumphant expressions turn to surprise as they lurch forward.
> (LS) Zoom out as 'B' is pulled into the mud.

The first treatment merely documents the event. The second allows the audience to participate in the action by focusing on the conflict, sharing the participants' feelings with the audience, and showing individual parts of the complete action.

Condensing action

Events in reality are often too long to sustain our interest. Three methods noted here can be used to condense action:

1) *The cut away.* To leave out unnecessary action, begin the activity (one person stringing a guitar), cut away (to the expectant look on child's face), then finish the action (show the final stage of stringing).

2) *The jump cut.* Show the beginning of an action (person walking down a long corridor), middle (person midway down the corridor), and end of the action (person arriving at door).

3) *Combination cut aways and jump cuts.* Show the beginning of a process, the middle (cutting away to show different parts of the action occurring at the same or different times), and end of the process.

Editing

Forms of editing

There are three major types of editing, the first requiring only the basic single system, the second and third necessitating two decks. With the *in-camera edit* scenes are planned ahead and shot in sequence, one added onto the other during taping. A scene can be erased and taped again by watching for the appropriate moment on the camera's monitor during playback. However, unless each scene is exactly the same length, a section cannot be replaced once the entire tape has been shot.

In *assemble editing* scenes are shot out of sequence, then assembled in the desired order. Filmmakers use this technique with one camera photographing all material that occurs in one location, then cutting the film to place the material at the points dictated by the script. The same effect could be acheived with in-camera editing, but it would mean taping in the first location, going to the second, back to the first, and so on. When the *insert edit* procedure is used, new material is edited into already existing material (parts of tape 'A' are editcd into the final tape, 'B').

Methods of editing

Rough or physical editing requires only demagnetized scissors and tape; electronic editing relies on two decks.

Physical editing. Splicing video tape by hand does not enable one to choose the exact frame, always results in a horizontal roll preceding the new picture with the new picture appearing at the top or bottom sweeping in to replace the old, and may result in recorder damage if the splice is not done correctly. Although momentarily distracting, the roll is acceptable and, without electronic facilities, is the only way to rearrange the tape once it has been shot. See Table 3.3 for directions.

TABLE 3.3: Splicing Video Tape

- Locate the two edit points (beginning and end of the segment) on the tape and cut.

- Overlap the ends that are to be joined approximately half an inch and cut at a 45 degree angle.

- Place the ends on a splicing block.

- Dab tape developer (iron carbonyl powder) on the ends of the segments to locate control tracks (spaced half an inch apart).

- Cut tape on one of the control pulses while it is lined up over the diagonal groove on the block. When both ends are cut along the control pulses, align edges.

• Tape on the nonoxide (dull) side only with a firm joint, leaving no space in between, and trim excess tape.

The roll accompanying the edit can be hidden by fading out (during taping) at the end of the previous scene, stopping, then fading in at the start of the next scene. The more regular in length all the scenes are, the less distracting the roll becomes. Try to edit where there is a repetitive sound (such as traffic) or no sound at all, to avoid a lag in audio. (Sound can also be dubbed in later.)

Electronic editing. This is a more precise method of editing tape. (The mechanics can be found in the literature accompanying the editing deck.) Try to edit pictures with sharp contrast. Every time a copy is made (referred to as the next "generation") some contrast is lost, and problems in the original tape will be amplified. If necessary, a tape can be recorded optically (off the monitor). Turn the volume on the VTR down to avoid extraneous sounds; lower the volume on the monitor to avoid feedback, then bring it up during the edit.

Transitions for one camera

Form, continuity, flow, balance and counterbalance between individual segments cannot be achieved without smooth transitions. The following techniques (Table 3.4) for moving from one scene to another do not require switching between cameras and are useful when editing in the camera.

TABLE 3.4: Single-Camera Techniques

1) Matching shots by motion. When a cut is used, a subject leaving the screen from the left in the previous shot must be seen entering the screen from the right during the next shot or the viewer will be disoriented. It is especially important to be aware of this if the tape will not be edited. Motion within a picture as well as action leaving a frame needs to be matched and provides flow, direction, and energy.

2) Matching shots by composition, according to continuity boards.

3) Fade out to black, change the scene or pan to a new subject, fade in. Can also be used to indicate the passage of time, end of a segment (chapter), or story.

4) Focus out (blur), focus in. Can be used to contract time, provide a feeling of unreality, uncertainty, or disorientation.

5) Indicate passage of time through dialogue, or fading music in and out. Music and sound effects can also be used as "leitmotifs" to unify a drama.

6) Begin each scene with a photograph, slide, drawing, or other graphic to establish mood, setting or passage of time.

7) Camera movement. (Pan or dolly back to reveal new elements or subjects of the next scene, and exclude the old action.)

8) Focus on foreground elements for the first scene, then tilt, zoom or dolly in to background subjects previously out of focus.

9) Blocking. The action itself leads the camera to the next scene.

10) Lighting. Areas previously obscured are revealed by turning up lights. This can also be used for flashbacks or flash forwards.

Plot

> *What is plot?* The plot of a story is the outlined pattern of action taken by a certain set of characters. This pattern must involve a central character—or characters—in a situation that appears to be hopeless. Then, after being brought into *conflict* with powerful forces—within himself, in others, or in Nature—the central character becomes enmeshed in certain *complications* which make the solving of his hopeless situation even more hopeless. He is forced to do—or not to do—certain things by the conflict-creating force. These things he is forced to do create a series of *crises* in his life—turning points in the story—which build up to a dramatic *climax*, which is the most important of the *crises*. This climax—resulting from the solving or from the not solving of the problems—resolves the story in that it brings the central character to the end of that particular episode in his life.[5]
>
> *Lewis Herman*

A list of plot patterns is given in Table 3.5.

TABLE 3.5: Plot Patterns

1. *Love pattern.* Boy meets girl, boy loses girl, boy gets girl.

2. *Success pattern.* The attempts of a person to achieve success.

3. *Cinderella pattern.* The ugly duckling is metamorphosed into a beautiful girl.

4. *Triangle pattern.* The interrelated loves of three protagonists.

5. *Return pattern.* The dramatic return of the prodigal son, the wandering father, the missing husband.

6. *Vengeance pattern.* The basic pattern for most murder-mystery stories. A crime is committed and vengeance must be wreaked on the criminal, whether by the forces of law and order, or by the person most affected by the crime.

7. *Conversion pattern.* The story of the reformation of an evil person. Conversions should be planned so that they grow out of the character into action, slowly and naturally.

8. *Sacrifice pattern.* Revolves around the actions of a person who, by sacrificing himself or his own personal aims, helps another to achieve some desired end.

9. *Family pattern.* "Family" interrelationships do not have to be among blood relations. The story can concern a group of people living together, insane asylum inmates, fellow travelers—any group of people thrown together by circumstances whose lives are brought to a dramatic point by those same circumstances.

SOURCE: Lewis Herman, *A Practical Manual of Screen Playwriting* (Cleveland, OH: World Publishing Co., 1963), pp. 33-34.

Notes

1. Anthony Garcia and Robert Myers, *Analogies: A Visual Approach to Writing* (New York: McGraw-Hill, 1974), p. 54.

2. John LeBaron and Louise Kanne, "Child-created Television in the Inner City," *Elementary School Journal* 75 (April 1975): 412.

3. Lewis Herman, *A Practical Manual of Screen Playwriting* (Cleveland, OH: World Publishing Co., 1963), p. 4.

4. Ibid., pp. 238-239.

5. Ibid., p. 31.

4

This End Up...
Graphics and Special Effects

"The image . . . is the most primitive form of symbolic function."[1]

Silvano Arieti

The most effective graphics are simple and direct, without being distracting or confusing. Preliminary sketches help students focus on essential elements, simplify reality and create a unified composition. The final graphic should reflect this same boldness and simplicity while incorporating basic principles of design and graphic communication (line, shape, balance, depth, harmony, texture, direction, pattern, emphasis, contrast) aimed at supporting the main idea of the graphic. When designing materials, be aware that black and white television reduces colors to a grey scale (white to dark grey).

Perspective

Understanding perspective will enable students to create more effective representational graphics as well as abstract designs, whether applied to titles, sets, advertising art, storyboards, diagrams or general classroom art activities.

To communicate a subject in two-dimensional space, these seven principles of perspective need to be considered: surface (objects further down—lower—on the paper appear to be closer); size (larger objects or parts of objects appear to be closer); surface lines (curved lines wrapping around part of an object suggest depth); overlapping (objects covering or crossing parts of other objects appear to be closer); shading (shading part of an object suggests depth); density (darker and more detailed objects or parts of objects add dimension and suggest nearness to the viewer); and foreshortening (flattened or oblong shapes representing surfaces

55

with symmetrical or parallel contours suggest depth—a cigar shape for a circle, or diamond shape for a square).[2]

Ask students to draw spheres, cones, and cubes (purchased from an art supply store or found in the environment) in a variety of positions and arrangements, and individually under different lighting conditions (using spotlights to highlight, change the apparent shape, depth and texture of the object and to create shadows). Follow up by looking at objects in the classroom and reducing them to spheres, cones and cubes. Practice drawing objects placed along parallel planes, lining up objects or parts of objects along northeastern or northwestern lines so that all elements point in the same direction.

Titles

Style

An effective title is thematically related to the material, matches the style of the production, attracts the viewer's attention and is directed toward an appropriate level for the audience. The layout and style of lettering should "sound" like and prepare the viewer for what follows. Try writing the same title in several different ways, reflecting its meaning or associations through its graphic notation. Read titles aloud using different attitudes (reflecting or contrasting their meanings), and draw them to represent the oral inflection.

Content

Writing titles becomes a language arts activity when they are used to summarize and communicate the main idea of a paragraph or story.

Size and lettering

An 11 x 14 inch posterboard card is the standard format (with a 9 x 12 inch usable space). Nonstandard sizes should still match the 4:3 screen ratio, with a minimum border area of one sixth of the total card. (In broadcast television, this area needs to be further reduced.) Since titles vary according to design, tonal contrast and size of letters, it is difficult to provide formulas. Generally, they should be no more than seven lines with letters one fifteenth of the screen height. Be certain the graphics are neat, clear, can be seen and read comfortably, and are centered—balanced within the television frame. Young students should be encouraged to letter their own titles. (They can use yellow paper with letters 1 to 1½ inches high.) For more professional needs any number of press or rub-on lettering kits, stencils, and spaghetti boards (rows of black felt with white press on letters) are available. If the title is typed, center it, double space to a maximum of six lines, and use capital letters (maximum of 32 per line). Draw with markers rather than crayons, and be certain letters are large enough to be seen when written on blackboards.

Displaying titles and other graphics

Titles can be mounted on an easel, or in a ring binder (stacked in reverse order, flipping down the new title over the old). A "crawl" (rolling titles on a continuous strip of paper attached to a cylinder or drum) can be made by cutting off the front of a cardboard box, putting two dowels through its sides, attaching a wide roll of paper inside with the titles printed on it, and rotating the dowels. Framed properly, the lettering will move slowly up or down the screen, depending upon which direction the dowels are turned. (The crawl can also be used as a teleprompter for an announcer, the talent, or "teacher" in an instructional lesson.) Titles can be printed and rolled on clear acetate placed between the camera and background so both visuals can be seen simultaneously, painted backwards on a sheet of glass and reflected in a tray of water, made to disappear by spelling out the title with styrofoam pellets and blowing them away (painting the pellets black helps reduce glare), or used in combination with the techniques outlined below.

Taping

Allow three times the normal reading speed when taping titles, and be certain lighting is diffused to avoid glare. If the camera is not set at the same height and exactly parallel to the title card, you will notice a "keystoning" effect. (Parallel lines no longer appear parallel, resulting in slanting letters.)

Sets

Design a set that is an extension of the title. Attach large, cut-out words to the walls; project words onto screens; make large cardboard placards of words such as fat, skinny, tall, hairy, and wide, appropriately drawn. Use the set to stimulate an instructional program on language arts.

Reveals and Animated Graphics

Numerous effects can be produced by sliding off black paper tabs to reveal a graphic below. For example, the sun and planets can be made to gradually appear by cutting out a stencil of the solar system from black paper, placing it over a sheet of white paper, and sandwiching small strips of black paper beneath the cut out areas. By pulling the strips out one at a time, the white paper will appear below, revealing the sun and planets.

Create an animated time line to move across the screen by pulling a strip of paper through two slits in a sheet of cardboard. Motion can be simulated in either a vertical or horizontal direction without the necessity of panning or tilting. (The distance between the graphic and lens would eventually increase, creating a keystoning effect.)

After orienting the viewer with an entire graphic, individual segments can be explored, analyzed, or shown at different points during the program. (Refer back to the framing exercises in Table 2.1.)

Produce a tape using student-made photographs or pictures from magazines. To achieve smooth transitions between photographs without stopping the camera or having to watch one picture flipped or slid over the next, place a black card to the right of the visual. Pan to the card, then back to the next visual which has been put in place during the transition. The photographs will appear to move on and off the screen from the left.

Rear Screen Projection

One way to provide a background without building a set or relocating is to project a scene or other illustration onto a translucent screen (oiled canvas, tracing paper, cloth, or a white plastic shower curtain two to three mills thick attached to a frame) from behind. Watch for hot spots or washing out the picture when lighting the area. Place slides in upside down only—not backwards—since they will be seen *through* the screen and not projected onto it. Because of the difference in speeds between tape and film, do not use a 16mm projector unless the projector has a variable speed adjustment.

Overhead Projection

Overhead projectors can create scenery, shadows, shapes, frames and abstract designs through the use of found objects, cardboard cutouts, drawings on transparencies or other acetate materials such as clear x-ray film or plastic wrap, projections of light through glasses filled with water or through clear vinyl filled with liquid shampoo or vegetable oil.

Other Materials

Depending upon program needs, a variety of other materials can be employed. (See Table 4.1.)

TABLE 4.1: Other Materials

- graphs
- strip or flip charts (to present information in a sequence)
- illustrated time lines (pan across, crawl, or reveal)
- diagrams
- slides (create your own transparencies by drawing, photographing, or lifting from magazines)
- stock footage from libraries
- maps and globes
- flannel clothboards
- pegboards for three-dimensional objects
- body cutouts
- puppets
- sandtables (topography, scale models)
- magnets (control from behind to add vertical motion; control from below for motion on a horizontal plane)
- real things (specimens, modified and unmodified objects; collections)
- models and miniature dioramas

Since depth of field will be severely limited, photograph the miniatures from an angle rather than head-on. Levers and manual controls can be added to create motion in two-dimensional graphics or three-dimensional scale models. Miniatures should be done to scale, placed within authentic settings, and in authentic arrangements. Some models may include life-size elements; if this is not the intention, avoid clues that reveal the true size of the miniature.

On-screen graphics have to be a reasonable size, balance with talent and set and, like words, can be extended into full-size sets—poster-size photographs, wall-size or three-dimensional topological maps, and so forth.

Special Effects

A large variety of studio effects, minus the elaborate equipment, can be modified for classroom use. Table 4.2 lists some.

TABLE 4.2: Special Studio Effects*

Snow. Bleach cornflakes, chop chicken feathers, drop some white confetti. It would be wise to cover the floor with a tarpaulin or sheet of plastic for easy cleanup.

Rain. Attach sprinkling cans to a strip of wood and tilt on cue. Best for outdoor use.

Fog. Blow steam from boiling water over dry ice, or place dry ice in water.

Cobwebs. Apply a thick layer of rubber cement between two boards. Pull apart to produce long strings of "cobwebs." Dust with talcum powder for heightened effect.

Automatic writing. Tape a piece of porous paper, such as newsprint, between two stands to create a screen. By standing behind the paper and writing or drawing with a black marker, the lines will miraculously appear without human aid. Remember to write in reverse. Illuminate from the front.

Fire. Blow paper or cloth flames with a fan. Convincing from a long shot only.

Wind. Large electric fans.

Blood, sweat and tears. Catsup for the former, a couple of drops of glycerin for the latter.

Gunshots. Fill a capsule from a decongestant with chocolate syrup, conceal in the hand, clutch at the appropriate part of the anatomy, and break the capsule. Messy, but effective.

Machine gun shots. Drill a series of holes in the set, cover from behind with black tape, focus a light on the tape, produce the sound and pull the tape off. The light seen through the holes will create the effect of machine gun fire.

Edibles. If you notice your food melting under the lights during a commercial, substitute the likes of mashed potatoes with food coloring for ice-cream, slices of bread and apricots for fried eggs, and cellophane for cracked ice.

Slow motion. Two decks are necessary. Use the slow motion adjustment on one deck to play the tape; use a second tape moving at normal speed to record it.

Stop action. Dub from one deck to another, using the still frame button. Useful for documentary, dramatic and instructional purposes to show part of an action. Music or narration can continue below.

*These and more complicated effects for the adventurous can be found in Rudy Bretz, *Techniques of Television Production* (New York: McGraw-Hill 1972) and Peter Weiner, *Making the Media Revolution* (New York: Macmillan, 1973).

Notes

1. Silvano Arieti, *Creativity: The Magic Synthesis* (New York: Basic Books, Inc., 1976). p. 39.

2. James Morrow and Murray Suid, *Media and Kids* (Rochelle Park, NJ: Hayden Book Company, Inc., 1977), pp. 46-47.

5

Pulses and Impulses...
Playing Games with Video

We have been talking about games, problems, acts of thought, and works of art as if
they were all alike. In certain basic essentials, *they are.*[1]

Anthony Garcia and Robert Myers

All students should have an opportunity to see themselves on the monitor and to look
through the monitor to see how it frames the world. It is important that each member of the
crew be familiar with all aspects of production in order to understand the capacities and
limitations of the VTR. As they become more involved in the process they will see how each
part contributes to the final product, be able to improve their own performances (thereby
improving the total work), to express more clearly what they want, and to suggest how to
accomplish it. Initial experiences should be enjoyable and not complicated by lengthy
explanations. A media vocabulary and aesthetic and technical considerations can be
introduced as the need arises. (Students will express these needs as they move naturally from
"play" through more structured to highly critical productions.)

Advise students to assume responsibility for equipment from the start. It is intended to be
used, but used with care. Repairs can be expensive and may disrupt their own or someone
else's shooting schedule for days.

Improvisational Games

The following improvisational games were chosen for their ability to quickly involve
students with and introduce them to the equipment, to help them become more comfortable in
front of the camera, and to develop the spontaneity necessary for creative taping in the studio
or street. The exercises are useful on several levels of learning. They provide a variety of visual,
aural and kinetic images to focus on (informally introducing different ways of selecting and

framing subjects); help focus attention on an activity rather than an extraneous source (whether in front of or behind the camera); quickly energize students; and encourage cooperation rather than competition. The exercises also strengthen skills in problem solving, reduce inhibitions and promote acting skills, and can be enjoyed and led by anyone—with or without previous experience in improvisation.

Introductions

Entire group, seated in a circle. Each person, in turn, introduces him or herself to the camera while watching the monitor. Say hello to the camera, have a dialogue with the monitor, tell a joke, say something about yourself or what you are experiencing at that moment, exaggerate the person you see on the screen, move in and out of the frame, introduce the next person. Pass the camera around the circle so that each person photographs the next. The exercise can be done without taping, or recorded and subsequently played back.

Object molding

Entire group, seated in a circle. The first student nonverbally "molds" an object from space (working with the space as if it really had substance), uses it, and passes it to the next person, who uses it again (maintaining size, shape, weight and texture). Pass the camera around the circle, concentrating on more detailed and less generalized images.

During playback, observe the space between your hands. Could you really see the object? Did you know what color it was? Would you be able to recognize the object if you had not been its creator?

Old hat, new hat

Entire group, seated in a semicircle. Each student, in turn, molds a hat from space, models it, passes it along to the next person who molds it into a new hat, and so on. Since the exercise is brief, one student should photograph the entire group. Do the exercise several times, avoiding repetition of styles. (The obvious ones will be exhausted quickly ... more inventive ones will follow.)

Emotional eyes

Pairs. 'A' is active, 'B' neutral. 'A' thinks of three different emotions (e.g., suspicion, confusion, surprise) and attempts to communicate them to 'B' using only the eyes (no forehead, eyebrows, nose or mouth—a book or sheet of cardboard can be held below the eyes if necessary), beginning from and returning to a neutral position after each emotion. 'B' tells 'A' what emotions he saw; 'A' then tells 'B' what emotions he was attempting to convey. Reverse roles; rotate camerapersons.

Mirror

Pairs, facing each other. One student assumes the role of leader, the other partner follows by exactly imitating (reflecting) the leader's movements (if the leader leans to the right, the other

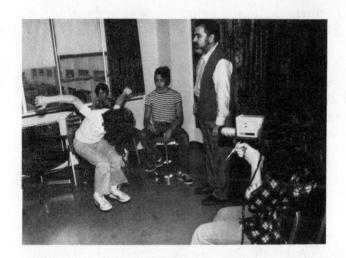

IMPROVISATIONAL GAMES help students to become comfortable and spontaneous in front of the camera. Here, students communicate through body movement in a series of panto-mimes.

person leans to the left). The leader may perform simple everyday activities, such as trying on clothes or washing a car, or may use abstract movements. Try to mirror everything including facial expressions, positions of the feet and body attitude.

Mirrors reduce students' self-consciousness by asking them to concentrate on their partners, not on the camera. Leaders should help their partners to move simultaneously, not try to trap or confuse them. Thinking about the camera, what they are doing, or the way they look will interfere with concentration and unison of movement. Additional problems may occur if students are mirroring too quickly. Ask them to slow down and use everyday activities if they are having trouble. In addition to reducing self-consciousness in front of the camera, mirrors develop physical awareness and coordination, and encourage participants to become more observant of themselves and others. Students operating the camera should begin to move through the class and around individuals to explore video's three-dimensional qualities.

Blind mirror

Pairs, facing each other, eyes closed. Partners begin with palms touching and perform a leaderless mirror (both partners initiating and following at the same time).

If students have difficulty performing a leaderless mirror, try the blind mirror alternating leadership. Did pairs feel they actually shared their movements, or did individuals feel manipulated (led) by each other? How did they feel about the game? Did it affect their concentration in any way? Players often express feelings of weightlessness or timelessness, or that a "third force" was directing their movements. Do they appear on tape as they expected to look? What kinds of movements evolved? Try points of contact other than hands (shoulders, backs, feet, elbows).

Watching a sport

Two groups. Each group decides on a sport to watch (horseracing, football, wrestling), and tries to communicate nonverbally what the sport is to the other group. There is no need to plan a scene or collaborate on what will happen—students watch the sport in their own individual ways within the security of the group.

Be certain students know that they are portraying *spectators*, not miming the sport itself. Students who are watching should wait until after the exercise to identify the sport. Students might want to follow up by taking a closer look at spectators' reactions on TV and how they differ at various sporting events.

This is an excellent exercise for loosening up even the shyest students. The group is, in effect, creating a scene without ever referring to the labels of "actor" or "actress." The exercise promotes positive interaction and laughter while providing a record of the scene for analysis if desired. For variation each group decides on something to eat, or a concert or lecture to attend.

Individual pantomimes

Entire group. In addition to the more familiar mimes such as tightrope walking, tug-of-war and walking on different surfaces, try strengthening concentration, observation and physical communication skills by working with variations on the use of a single object. For example, ask students to pick up an imaginary wheelbarrow and wheel it across the room; fill it with apples and wheel it on a bumpy road; fill it with feathers and wheel it on a windy day.

Gibberish incident

Pairs. One partner tries to communicate an incident or brief story to the other using gibberish (nonsense syllables) and accompanying physical expression. No real words are permitted. Remind partners to reverse roles.

Gibberish is an excellent way of energizing, animating and loosening up students both vocally and physically, and encourages participants to discover new ways of communicating nonverbally.

Join the activity

Entire group. One student begins a physical activity involving an object (throwing a blanket onto the sand, jumping rope, painting a wall). As each student recognizes what the object/activity is, he enters and joins the activity by actually doing it or linking up in some other way—pushing dirt back into a hole someone else is digging; helping dig the same hole; entering with a derrick; digging another hole; tunneling into the first. Students can talk *about* what they are doing, but should not *tell* what they are doing. They should communicate through body movement rather than simply describe action with words. Feedback focuses on how accurately the activity was expressed, on the clear use of space objects, and on finding ways for individuals to contribute to a group activity already in progress.

Moving an object

Small groups. Each group (independently) decides on a large object to move (simply agreeing upon the object and nothing else) and proceeds to move it, trying to communicate what it is to the other groups. Students may discuss the process of moving the object but may not name it or any of its parts directly. To begin, all grab the object simultaneously without determining who will carry what. (Part of the problem involves adjusting to each other spontaneously in order to make the scene believable.) Feedback should focus on how clear the object was, what qualities of the object were communicated, if the object maintained its size, shape and weight throughout the improvisation (objects do not tend to expand or contract greatly in reality), and how well the group resolved its conflicts.

Object moving you

Small groups. Proceed as above, determining an object that will move the group (air balloon, roller coaster, revolving barrel in a fun house).

Explosive mirror

Pairs. 'A' initiates a series of sound and movement combinations, freezing after each combination. 'B' attempts to mirror the combination as simultaneously as possible. 'A' does not have to relate combinations in any way, and should move spontaneously without planning positions. When mirroring, move with the opposite side of the body. Leaders should want to challenge their partners, but not perform combinations so quickly that the exercise cannot be accomplished. If 'B' is not alert or concentrating completely on 'A', he will not be able to mirror simultaneously.[2]

Orchestra

Entire group. One student volunteers to be the conductor; the remaining group becomes the orchestra. The conductor moves, using his entire body to conduct; the orchestra responds by making corresponding sounds. The conductor then directs sounds toward the orchestra; the orchestra moves in response. The orchestra does not need to coordinate its efforts—each student improvises individually within the group.[3]

Abstract machines

Entire group, standing in a circle. One person enters the circle and begins a repeatable sound and movement combination with a machine-like quality and continues while someone enters with another combination that "links up" with the first. Continue until everyone has entered and the entire group has formed a machine-like unit.

Students should focus on machine-like qualities rather than on creating a specific machine. Although two parts could enter simultaneously, it is preferable to add only one part at a time since each person is contributing a new and possibly unexpected element to the machine that will need to be incorporated by the next person to enter. For variation, students create a "monster" in a similar manner.[4]

Notes

1. Anthony Garcia and Robert Myers, *Analogies: A Visual Approach to Writing* (New York: McGraw-Hill, 1974), p. 65.

2. Adapted from Don Kaplan, "How to Tickle a Whale and Other Everyday Activities," *Music Educators Journal* 64 (October 1977): 27-28.

3. Ibid., p. 27.

4. Ibid., p. 31.

6

Receivers and Transformers...
Producing Instructional Video

The bulk of schoolroom video has been educational TV, homemade imitations of network TV. Like a teacher-dominated lecture, such programs tend to overwhelm all student response, pouring out over a class like a static-filled blanket.[1]

Jonathan Price

In *Video-Visions* Jonathan Price describes how educators learned from successful business-men to build instructional models based on "ideal" patterns. Lessons were structured to elicit programmed responses, allowing students to imitate models without being "sidetracked" by discussions or personal opinions.

It is easy to use television as a preacher-teacher; the technology of the VTR makes it an ideal medium for instructional design. It sees and hears, it records, it plays back (a closed circuit with no interference). Teachers need set up demonstrations only once, can play them back many times, and are free to give viewers individual attention while the tape is played. Television can show a single action from a variety of viewpoints, two parts of the same action occurring simultaneously in the same or different places, or the condensation of lengthy events into a few moments' time. Instead of asking students to view a small object or procedure individually, it can be televised live (in close-up) through monitors or played back on tape for the entire class to see at once. Master classes, resource people from other communities, and courses which could otherwise not be taught become readily available. A tape can be made on location some distance from the school. Sound effects can be used to heighten viewer interest and describe, support or comment upon the visual images. Live action combines with slides, film, models and graphic displays.

Simply recording and playing back an established model is not the only approach. A class can conceive, research, organize, develop and produce instructional materials for itself or for younger students and prepare for televised lessons by writing step-by-step books of instructions and visualizing ideas through storyboards. When used in a student-centered manner, taped lessons are a means for identifying and dealing with children's own problems, combining both cognitive and affective areas of learning. Tapes can be revised and updated easily, used for training other students, shared within the school and district, played on cable television and made available between school systems. Even nationwide exchange programs of student-produced tapes become possible.[2]

The Tube has its advantages for imitative learning, but can also induce sleep in the most attentive viewer. Simply showing a procedure on television does not ensure that any communication has occurred. It is thus necessary to provide for as much viewer interaction as possible. Use the "stop" and "pause" buttons, ask what the next step should be ... what would happen if.... Provide time for questions, reactions, and note-taking. Show a part of a lesson, ask the class if the right materials were used in the correct order, start the tape again and show the results of its decision. If a skill needs to be imitated, be certain the technique is understood and provide opportunities for individual modification and opportunities for teaching the skill to other students.

Guidelines

The following list of guidelines is not a rigid, prescriptive "recipe." It is designed to help students develop skills in organizing and communicating their ideas, and to clarify what student video producers will be learning by creating their own lessons.

Preparation

Objectives and needs

Keeping goals to a minimum, establish the specific behavioral objectives you expect to achieve.[3] Outline the kinds of change that will occur, what the lesson will enable viewers to do that they could not do before, what skills students will develop, and how they will be able to demonstrate them. Which objectives can best be achieved by using the VTR?

Audience

Identify who will use the lesson (age, subject knowledge). Are there any words or terms used in the production that need to be defined? What is the attitude toward the subject likely to be? If the audience is young or not likely to be highly interested or motivated, provide for more viewer interaction.

Content outline

Determine the content of the lesson by researching, gathering materials, and extracting the most important elements. Choose learning experiences that will best achieve the goals and write a brief outline listing the topics to be covered.

PROGRAM PLANNING. Students and teacher discuss goals and methods, while cameraman learns to handle his equipment before actual shooting begins.

Treatment

Determine the style or combination of styles or presentation that will best communicate the objectives (lecture, lecture/demonstration, panel or interview). There is no reason why an informative program cannot be presented in an entertaining or dramatic format. However, anything that distracts from achieving the goals will weaken the lesson's effectiveness.

Decide on the specific visual and aural materials (titles, charts, models, diagrams, sound and music) and the optical effects necessary to illustrate and reinforce concepts.[4] Visuals and camera movement should be direct, simple and motivated by the goals of the lesson.

If there is no visual interest, the lesson should probably be recorded on audio tape.

Scripting

Continuity

Refer back to the content outline and identify main points and subpoints. It is helpful to write each one on an index card; organize and reorganize in a storyboard manner until the proper sequence is obtained. Be certain the sequence is logical (skills organized developmentally in an action-reaction or causal relationship).

Pacing

Be aware of the overall balance and pacing of the lesson. Determine how much time each point should take; provide variety and pace slowly for difficult parts; and avoid emphasizing subpoints at the expense of major ones. The lesson should sustain and, if possible, build interest by driving toward main points. Determine where any viewer interaction will occur. (The time can be provided for in the tape itself by leaving a visual on the screen.)

Reviews

Does the nature of the lesson suggest periodic review? To focus attention, a brief review of material covered elsewhere may be included in the introduction. There might be one review summarizing main points at the end or one review in the middle of the lesson and one at the end. Determine the amount of reinforcement by the complexity of the lesson.

Final production plan

Choose a form of storyboard and/or script that best serve the material being presented and communicates it most clearly to the director, actors and technicians.

Talent

Formal scripts may inhibit students without previous acting experience. Unless a voice-over is used, a simple outline with cue sentences should be sufficient. If the talent (anyone who appears in front of the camera) is completely familiar with the content of the lesson, a few cues will enable him or her to speak naturally and comfortably about the subject. Direct the talent to share information with the audience, not to "talk down" to it; any attitudes of boredom, insincerity or lack of interest will be projected to the viewer. Advise the talent to speak conversationally—phrasing, punctuating, expressing and pausing as he or she would in actual conversation, to look at the camera (maintaining eye contact with the audience), and to adjust his or her pacing to fit. Working from cues rather than formal scripts will encourage students to use their own words and develop individual patterns.

Instructional guides

To clarify materials and methods for others and reinforce concepts for themselves, student producers may want to design instructional guides to accompany the tapes. Guides should list objects clearly, concisely, and in the order in which they are introduced. Include any materials (background reading, texts, vocabulary, concepts, equipment, diagrams) that are new or need to be reviewed before playing the tape; and explain how the lesson relates to the total curriculum.

Playing the tape does not guarantee that learning has taken place. Provide questions that will enable students to demonstrate the effectiveness of the tape (i.e., to translate what they have seen into actual practice, to find out if communication between television emitter and student receiver has occurred, to enable students to identify what has changed, and to lead students into more focused activities in the same or related areas). Label tapes carefully including *grade level, subject area, and nature of the lesson.*

Evaluation

The evaluation process will give producers information concerning the value of the tape for a particular audience, the problems in its design, and the adequacy of the objectives. Critiques are important so that students can evolve standards of quality.

Did the lesson achieve its goals? Were objectives clearly presented and at a level appropriate to the audience? Was the subject matter relevant, accurate, developed logically, and interestingly presented? Did the lesson hold the viewer's attention? Stimulate discussion? What topics were of the greatest and least interest? Could more viewer interaction be developed? Was sufficient time provided for written and/or verbal response? Was the lesson well paced? Graphic materials clearly visible? Were there technical problems or artistic elements that distracted from or were irrelevant to the goals of the lesson? Was there a strong introduction and adequate summary? Did the talent appear natural and interested and maintain eye contact with the viewer? What did his nonverbal attitude communicate?

Validation

If you plan to share the lesson with other classes, return to the production phase to modify materials if objectives were not met during pilot testing. Any errors should be corrected and reevaluated. Was there adequate pre- and post-testing? Is the lesson consistently effective from classroom to classroom and school to school?

LITERATURE COMES TO LIFE for young students in a video production of *The Three Musketeers.*

Suggested lessons

Instructional uses for video are unlimited. Almost any subject can be researched, learned and presented in video format. In particular, many processes and procedures, techniques and skills lend themselves especially well to video presentations. You can dramatize historic events or scenes from literature, demonstrate experiments, show how equipment is operated. Following are a number of specific suggestions, but don't stop with them!

1. In biology or other science classes, basic laboratory techniques can be demonstrated by the teacher on video tape. Student experiments can be taped and then discussed with the class. You may want to experiment with video techniques by shooting a lesson on frog dissection, for example, into an overhead mirror. (This results in a natural—although reversed—viewpoint). Or you can tape microscopic organisms through a microscope (see Figure 6.1).

2. The old "show and tell" lessons can be made more interesting and lasting through video

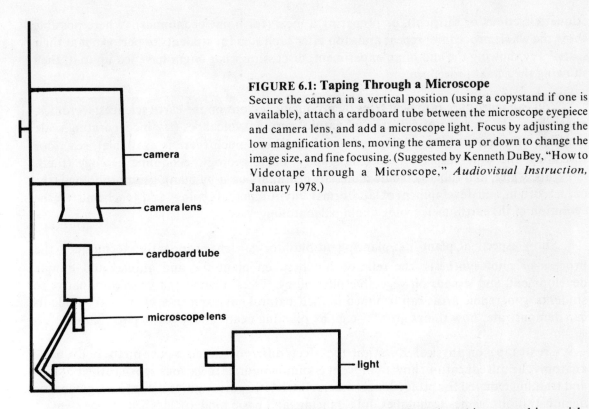

FIGURE 6.1: Taping Through a Microscope
Secure the camera in a vertical position (using a copystand if one is available), attach a cardboard tube between the microscope eyepiece and camera lens, and add a microscope light. Focus by adjusting the low magnification lens, moving the camera up or down to change the image size, and fine focusing. (Suggested by Kenneth DuBey, "How to Videotape through a Microscope," *Audiovisual Instruction*, January 1978.)

tape. Students can demonstrate hobbies and interests such as building things, working with ceramics, or performing dance steps for the camera, enabling the rest of the class to see the program once or many times, and for everyone to get a "front seat."

3. Video can help the teacher demonstrate vocal inflections, lip movements and body gestures of foreign languages. Words and parts of speech can be dramatized.

4. You can develop affective skills by dramatizing incidents that teach respect for differences among individuals—such as physical handicaps, regional accents, values, opinions, or ideas. Show situations in which an individual tries to overcome an obstacle (such as an architectural barrier).

5. As has been said before, video is ideal for demonstrating equipment. It can show how to use equipment in the laboratory, machinery for vocational training, apparatus in physical education, film projectors, or a video tape recorder. Show an illustration of the equipment with each part clearly labeled (and correctly spelled), briefly explain the use or function of each part in sequence (using the word in a sentence), the preparation of any materials that are used with the equipment, and the complete operation of the equipment. The lesson can become interactive by providing each student with his or her own equipment (or diagram) to refer to, or giving students a drawing of each part or step on a separate card to be properly sequenced or arranged, like a puzzle, to form the complete unit.

6. Demonstrate a process or procedure—e.g., using library facilities (card catalogs, microfilm), producing audiovisual materials (including lettering and layout), a lesson on

etiquette (serious or satirical), or preparing a meal (for home economics). Where possible show the whole procedure; repeat and stop after each step for students to perform it at their seats.[5] Try showing the end of an experiment, discussing what might have led up to it, then showing the actual procedure.

7. You can reproduce rare field trips by producing lessons on the earth sciences: tectonics, mineralogy, the creation of geysers and natural springs, volcanoes (try incorporating scale models), oil retrieval (where oil comes from and how much there is available), sea floor spreading and other aspects of oceanography, lunar geology, economic geology (fuels, minerals, water, and other geologic materials profitably used by man), geomorphology (the nature, origin, and development of landforms), environmental geology and geochemistry, the evolution of the earth, meteorology, and paleontology.

8. Show aspects of plant life: planting an outdoor garden, propogation techniques, the process of photosynthesis, the relationship between plant life and animal and human development, and lessons on vegetable physiology. Trees, plants, and vegetation native to students' geographic areas can be taped in their natural environments; elementary students can demonstrate "how things grow"—e.g., by planting beans and seeds in paper cups.

9. Create tapes on physical education: the effects different exercises have on the body, basic anatomy, health education, how to prevent common injuries in various sports, athletic skills and training required for professional careers (interview sports figures if possible), gymnastic demonstrations, games techniques, folk dancing, and basic modern/classical dance steps.

10. Create tapes on driver education: identifying traffic signs (a useful introduction to shapes for younger students), preventing injuries (the importance and use of seat belts), a consumer's guide to automobile safety—which manufacturers design the safest cars (including current and future safety devices), "rules of the road," what to do if the car breaks down, and information concerning automobile club services and insurance. Simulate and tape causes of common accidents and how they can be prevented (perhaps using the camera in a subjective role—the audience "seeing" through the eyes of the driver). Stage and tape an "accident" using the hidden camera technique (local organizations or parent volunteers may be able to arrange a safe simulation). Ask "lawyers" to prepare cases for the plaintiff and defendant, select witnesses (people who were unaware of the taping at the time of the "accident"), choose a "jury," and conduct a "trial" using the participants' testimony first, then the tape as final evidence. (How did the participants' and witnesses' stories compare with the actual event?) An entire series of tapes on driver education—from learning how to drive and prepare for the road test to purchasing a car and maintaining it—could be produced and circulated within the school district.

11. Demonstrate basic principles of physics and mechanics: machines (the lever, pulley, wheel and axle, inclined plane, wedge, and screw), energy, force, power, gravity and gravitation, weight, equilibrium, Newtonian laws, and the application of these principles to human movement.

12. Produce lessons on special education: rehabilitation techniques and services, programs for students and adults with special needs. physical activities for the disabled and elderly,

DANCE, EXERCISE AND PHYSICAL EDUCATION classes lend themselves **particularly well to video taping.** (Photo: Peter Krupenye.)

communication techniques and electronic information systems, methods for helping blind people see and deaf people hear.

13. Encourage guidance and career studies. Counselors provide basic information and students prepare tapes on financial aid, college admissions procedures, and using the guidance center. Presentations by college representatives can be taped and shown schoolwide. Students can show "their day at the job"—placing themselves at a particular occupation in the actual setting, wearing appropriate clothing, and performing the actual functions required. Information can be provided on local businesses and industries through guided tours of company operations and interviews with personnel (how they feel about the company or corporation, how supervisors feel about employees and employees about employers); a mock corporation structured in the classroom; government jobs explored through on-site interviews with officials; and tapes prepared on how to interview for a job. In both general and special education settings, students should role play and improvise scenes on different occupations, then compare their impressions to tapes showing the actual situations.

Plan a tape on cultural anthropology; include definitions, interviews, information on leading anthropologists, examples of what individual entering this field might be expected to do, what they might expect to accomplish, and what prominent discoveries have increased the public's attention to the field (e.g., King Tutankhamen).

Compile a list of jobs in television based upon what students think are available and those that actually exist. Research and include information such as:

- what occurs on a typical day
- amount of freedom or supervision
- equipment used
- how individual jobs contribute to the total production
- salary, hours, and benefits
- educational background, special skills, or physical requirements
- personal interests and temperament appropriate for the job
- opportunities for advancement
- advantages and disadvantages compared to similar positions in other mass media fields (especially those in film)

The portapak itself stimulates instructional lessons on its mechanics, processes and related areas (Table 6.1).

TABLE 6.1: Instructional Lessons on (and with) the Portapak

- optics (including persistence of vision)
- electricity (alternating and direct current)
- principles of magnetic fields and electromagnets
- acoustics (process of hearing and sound transmission)
- recording techniques, microphones and sound amplification
- magnetic and optical sound systems (how sound gets onto tape or film and how it is "read")
- how the picture gets from the camera to the monitor: how the vidicon tube works; how the

picture tube works; how the VTR heads function; the role of the sync pulse; conversion of light into electrical and magnetic signals
- training student technicians; building and repairing equipment, making connections and plugs, troubleshooting and maintenance, establishing standards of performance
- editing techniques
- special effects (e.g., creating fog, and relating it to weather conditions)
- lighting (e.g., shadows, and relating them to eclipses and day/night cycles)
- selecting equipment lighting sources—incandescent, carbon arc, fluorescent, quartz)
- methods of broadcasting (transmission and reception)
- cassette and cartridge innovations
- related areas such as photocopying and developing; licensing and broadcast standards; forms of energy; building a crystal radio set; how still photography works (from the camera obscura to present day 35mm photography); comparing video, audio, and computer tapes

Notes

1. Jonathan Price, *Video-Visions* (New York: Plume/New American Library, 1977), p. 29.

2. There are three levels of media production: creative-inventive, adaptive, and imitative, and the reader is referred to Brown, Lewis, and Harcleroad, *Audiovisual Instruction,* pp. 80-81 for more thoughts on this. All three levels help students clarify objectives, develop self-discipline, and use their imaginations.

3. As defined by Hilgard and Bower *(Theories of Learning),* there must be a behavioral change in an organism in order for learning to occur.

4. Most special effects such as slow, fast, and reverse motion require two VTRs—one to create the effect, the other to dub the effect onto. Descriptions of these techniques can be found in Peter Weiner's *Making the Media Revolution: A Handbook for Video-Tape Production* (New York: Macmillan, 1973).

5. The jump cut can be used when showing the complete action is unnecessary. For a demonstration of bookbinding, for example, it would not be especially enlightening to show every stitch being made... show the begininning, jump to the middle, then to the end of the process.

7

After Image . . .
Future Studies on Video

All education springs from some image of the future. If the image of the future held by
a society is grossly inaccurate, its education system will betray its youth.[1]

Alvin Toffler

Technology and social change are outracing the educational system. According to Billy
Rojas, there is an "overspill from the future that is pouring into the present,"[2] and it is
important that educators show students the nature of change, growth and adaptation.

The process of predicting the future involves fundamental educational goals—the same
goals already encountered in other areas of video study. Creating future scenarios on video
tape enables students to develop analytical skills within an experiential format, to manipulate
materials systematically, to learn traditional disciplines from a variety of directions in a
manner which relates directly to their lives, and to discover ways in which they can alter or
affect the world they will be in.

Future studies are interdisciplinary and ask basic questions about life—what our needs are,
what needs to be done, and what's worth doing. The student and his or her community are the
centers of learning and one center affects another. Individual areas become, by necessity,
integrated, and videotape can play an important role in the integration. "To understand any
group of people, a commune or global community, one needs the analytical tools provided by
psychology, sociology, social psychology and whatever else can be brought to bear."[3] The
investigation becomes a kaleidoscopic vision. Television (a "new" technology itself already
multidisciplinary in nature) is used to study individual subjects, each subject seen from

different perspectives, at different times, overlapping with other subjects and rooted in the past and present. According to Michael McDaniel, education becomes a problem of overchoice: "There is so much that *could* be taught that it is almost impossible to decide what *should* be taught."[4]

From this abundance of futuristic images, two major concerns emerge. Many youngsters— and some adults—are unable to see themselves as the cause of their actions. Someone or something else (a person, the world, a deity or devil) is always acting upon them; they are mere victims of circumstance. Investigating futures reinforces connections (logically and ethically considered) between means and ends; what we do today affects tomorrow on a personal, interpersonal or global level. Once students assume responsibility for their actions they can exert greater control over themselves, their education and their interactions with others.

In addition to cause-effect consciousness, future studies help students integrate and control fragments of information and develop new constructs by selecting from a variety of old sources. Students become "unstuck" in time; they prepare themselves for changes by seeking alternatives, finding new ways to solve problems, and analyzing their values and making better choices.

The future cannot be predicted without confronting the past and present, and forecasting requires creativity, research and methodical thinking. Predictions do not have to be correct for learning to have occurred; the *process* of thinking about causes and effects enables students to anticipate and cope with change.

What follows are specific suggestions for activities with "future" orientations. Many, of course, can be used in traditional subject areas. The student gains from the analysis of issues, and the creation of video tapes, and he/she prepares for the future.

Applications and Guidance Studies

Careers

By investigating future occupations, students become familiar with a variety of potential roles and possibilities other than those received from family, friends and television. Many questions confront students. What jobs are likely to evolve? Which will become obsolete? Will there always be a need for artists? auto mechanics? teachers? Will money still be a career goal or will other values become more important?

Communications

What overlapping has occurred between print and electronic journalism (e.g., magazine format and investigative reporting) on television? How does television news compare with print? How have newspaper formats changed and what new formats may occur in the future? Study recent editorial policy and predict the future policy of a magazine. How will the role of libraries change to accommodate new formats? What effects do cultural differences have on communications between races (ethnocentricity) and countries, and how might they affect attitudes toward extraterrestrial life?

Education

What new forms of teaching are developing? Will learning machines, computerized information systems, and televised courses replace human teachers? Is the educational marketplace expanding or shrinking? Why? Will colleges have to continue advertising for students? Will "university without walls," work-study, and extension programs replace the campus as centers of education? (High school students might want to investigate these types of programs at various colleges and document their findings on tape.)

Values and religion

Can you establish a values system for the entire universe? What will people value in the future? Based upon these values, invent a new version of heaven and hell: dramatize and tape a futuristic version of Dante's inferno and purgatory, and interview "souls" who were sent there. What punishment is inflicted on those who break moral codes? What are the rewards of heavenly bliss? Televise a panel discussion on the forms evil takes today, what might represent evil in a future society, and recent changes in religious institutions. Why have beliefs and practices been able to remain the same for centuries in certain societies? Will they be able to remain static? What predictions can you make based on heightened American interest in Oriental religious systems? Invent a new religion to meet future needs and promote it through one minute, 30-second, and 15-second commercials.

The law

What kinds of cases will lawyers be trying at the end of the century? Will the protection of privacy become an increasing problem? Dramatize and tape a trial concerning a future offense (e.g., a psychosurgical error or cloning violation), and have the class decide the outcome. Enact cases occurring in a 21st century divorce court. Tape discussions on what prisons will be like in the future and how you would attempt to rehabilitate political or social offenders. Dramatize the crime of the 22nd century.

Political science

Discuss what would happen if there were five times as many people in your classroom as there are now. Turn on the VTR, fill a small space with a large crowd and one chair, and document negotiations for space and comfort. Convene and record a Global Planning Council with individuals representing different planets and different ideologies. Prepare and present proposals; negotiate agreements concerning outer space, travel, boundaries, immigration, nuclear plants, peace and security arrangements (use contemporary concerns as a basis for futuristic concerns). Or: The polar caps have melted and there is only a small mass of land left on earth to hold the world's population. As representatives of different countries, how could you best use severely limited resources to support the current population and insure enough food and space for future generations? How could you use the vast bodies of water to advantage? Share the resulting tape with other classes for feedback and additional discussion.

Television

Predict what future television programming will be like. How do the situation comedies of the past compare with sit-coms of the present? Produce an episode taking place in the future (include homes, clothing, furniture, and kitchens), and role play the nuclear family (discuss affective responses to the experience). What will people be laughing at? Choose another television genre—look at an episode written 15 years ago and tape a scenario for one to be transmitted 10 years in the future.

Sociology

How does the way women and men are portrayed on television prepare them for roles in society? Have several television crews interview one another and people outside the school concerning sex roles and expectations; analyze the tapes and chart different attitudes according to male/female respondents, by generation, and by profession. How many women see themselves in a liberated role? Do attitudes change from profession to profession (i.e., are women treated differently in different occupations)? Combine statistics, interviews, and supportive materials (TV commercial footage that promotes negative or stereotyped images) into a video documentary focusing on past, present, and possible future sex roles. What are the implications for marriage and human liberation?

Anthropology

Discussing our limitations and prejudices enables us to develop more imaginative possibilities. Tape interviews with students to discover ways in which we duplicate existing (and inherited) prejudicial behavior patterns. To what extent has your own future been determined by when, where, and to whom you were born? Prepare an instructional lesson demonstrating how circumstances of birth determine futures in other countries and have done so in previous civilizations. Do we now or will we ever have a caste system in America? Interview parents to determine how they imitate their parents; tape a panel discussion exploring what parental qualities students admire, which they would like to see changed, and which they actually imitate. Are children growing up with the same attitudes as their parents, or are attitudes changing?

Possible, probable, and preferable futures

Possible futures are imaginative: they could occur, but are not likely to. Probable futures are defined as events that are likely to occur, and are forecasted by examining conflicts already happening. Preferable futures are arrived at through values clarification, and are linked to values that underlie social and personal choice.[4] Choose one aspect of the future and dramatize it on tape in three ways—as possible, probable, and preferable futures.

Science

Videotape scenes and panel discussions about the scenes on how our lives will be affected by scientific developments and their implications. Subjects for dramatization and discussion may include:

- Genetic engineering (determining what characteristics a person will have). Who chooses? What problems could be eliminated by genetic control? If we could control our evolution, how would we want to evolve?

- Cloning. Who decides who gets cloned? Dramatize the diary of a clone.

- Organ transplants. How would you feel receiving the heart of a pig if it meant saving your life? Would you donate an organ to someone else? Would you allow organs to be transplanted to another person after you die? Would you clone for organ transplants?

- Cyborgs and sophisticated robots. Would they match the image of their makers? How human should they be? What would you have them do? Would they replace people at jobs? What good or bad effects would this have?

- Time travel by "freezing" people. Would you take the risk?

- Artificial intelligence. Would you accept the implantation of memory cells from a student who has already learned a particular subject? What would be the positive and negative effects of taking a pill for reading? How would this affect the education system?

- Using computers to make political decisions.

- Developing synthethic foods and ocean farming.

- Controlling the weather. How can the weather be controlled? What negative effects might this have? What would be the impact on urbanization and topology?

- Artificial life. Would a person conceived, born, and grown outside the body be "human"? Subject to the same moral values as the rest of us? Who would be its family? What would you put on its "birth" certificate?

- Animal communications. Do you think human/animal communications are worth pursuing? How would you feel conversing with a monkey through sign language? Would "talking with the animals" make you feel less human or superior?

- Biofeedback (monitoring and controlling your involuntary bodily functions). What effect would the widespread use of this technique have on the medical profession?

- Psychosurgery. Who is responsible if something goes wrong? Would you trust someone who is about to alter your brain? How would using electrical stimulation to reduce anxiety or depression be preferable to taking pills? What would happen if a "mad scientist" or political leader decided to use psychosurgery to create an army of people completely subservient to him? Would have surgery performed on criminals to remove aggression and selected emotions? What crimes would qualify for this treatment? Do anger, rage, anxiety, depression, or aggression serve a useful purpose? Dramatize a society where these emotions have been eliminated.

- Future implications for drugs, alcohol, tobacco, and the legalization of marijuana.

- Colonizing other planets. Plan a colony on another planet. What values would you impose? Moral standards? What would be "just"? Beautiful? What would the government be like?

How would you deal with non-conformity and individualism within the system. Determine the physical conditions of the planet—how could you put these to use for the benefit of the people? What animals would you take with you? Works of art? Video tapes? Books? Would you use any of the techniques listed above—i.e., mind control, artificial intelligence, cloning—within the colony? Would you have "test tube babies" fertilized on earth implanted in women on the planet? Who would be the real mother?

Video reports on the current status of any of these areas can be presented as an alternative to scenes and panel discussions.

Neighborhoods

Interview residents to determine how your neighborhood has changed during the last five years; during the last 15 years. Have the changes been beneficial or detrimental? When did the most rapid changes occur? Join and videotape activities that can have a positive effect on your neighborhood (such as youth and community centers, drug rehabilitation programs, urban renewal programs). Report on how frequently people relocated 25 years ago, 50, and 150 years ago. How often has your own family moved? How will increasing rates of transience affect home life, friendships, and the feeling of a neighborhood? What is the future of the ghetto?

Transportation

Produce a video report on what will get people from here to there in the year 2025. What environmental problems will new modes of transportation cause or solve? Do a report about how automobiles have changed, what new designs are in progress, and what they might look like in the future. Which modes of transportation will become obsolete and what new ones (e.g., roadless vehicles) will develop? What is the likelihood of you or your children taking space shuttles to the moon or vacationing on distant planets? Will you ever see pollutionless transportation? Will train and boat travel become obsolete? Could you foresee the return of blimps? How does the proportion of time spent traveling now compare with time spent during the turn of the century? In previous centuries? How quickly has that time contracted during the 20th century in comparison to previous centuries? During the last 20 years? How has the availability or lack of transportation to your own community affected that community's growth? The growth of other cities?

Urbanization

Report on the development of your city from its inception to its present condition. Predict the future of the city based on population trends, preferable and available locations, and topography. Include photographs, charts, and graphs in the tape to support your predictions. How will concepts of work change and what new services will be provided? What effect will staggered work weeks have on transportation? Diet? Banking hours? Design and videotape a guided tour of the ideal city (created in miniature). Design scale-model living spaces using geodesic dome kits, and record a discussion on the effects different spaces have on human beings. Design urban dwellings for creatures on another planet. Tape a panel of urban representatives, each member presenting evidence to support his or her city as the city of the future (e.g., Chicago, New York, Philadelphia, San Francisco, Houston).

Extended life span

Tape a panel on unlimited life span. Are extended life spans good or bad? What effect would they have on population growth? Natural resources? Intergenerational relations? Family planning? Would they expand the "generation gap" or contract it by allowing several generations to exist together? Would incest become acceptable? What effect would extended lives have on the government? Laws? Social customs? Write a video drama around the theme of immortality.

Television news of the future

Using current affairs as a basis, predict and televise the news of the future. What are countries fighting about and what are the prospects for war and peace? How violent is the society of the future and what forms does violence take? What is terrorism like in the 21st century? How have race and foreign relations improved or deteriorated? What changes in international relations have been necessitated by diminishing world resources? How have races from other planets been treated? What items will consumers prefer? Will ecology affect consumer preference? Marketing techniques? Packaging? What will the Ralph Naders of the future be investigating? How have political affairs, urban problems, energy sources, technology, economics, the division of labor, and national health insurance developed? How are disadvantaged countries using technology to compete with the major powers? How are multinational corporations preventing the people of disadvantaged countries from advancing? What animals have become extinct and which are endangered? What problems is change causing (e.g., what occurs when leaders try to modernize tradition-bound societies)? What is easy or difficult to change? What is likely to always remain the same? What is future America like? What songs are being sung? Select a specific year and speculate on what etiquette will be like, how the federal budget will be spent, and devote a portion of the broadcast to reviews of the latest films and books. Send a news team to cover a governmental agency spending its budget as it considers blue and white collar workers, urban and suburban dwellers, and picketing citizens groups. Report on the event from several viewpoints: compare each subjective report to the objective occurrence. What new products are likely to emerge and new techniques to market them? Which "old" products will still be sold (e.g., what is the future of bubble gum)? How would holography affect television productions and advertising?

Science fiction

Write, dramatize, and tape science fiction scripts. Record alternate endings to established science fiction stories, or develop productions based on common themes in science fiction literature (e.g., humanity's loss of control to machines). Try to convert people from one planet to the ideologies of another; choose a specific date in the future, determine what life will be like then, and televise a science fiction program taking place in the future-future. Is science-fiction "now" different from science-fiction "then"? Which fictions have become facts?

Interviews

Videotaped interviews (see Chapter 9) are another resource for future studies. Interview:

• Archaeologists who have found the ruins of our civilization. What accurate information or misconceptions might they infer? What contributed to our demise?

•A person made entirely from organ transplants. How common are the various transplants? Can you pick and choose from an organ display? Are organs donated by humans or made from plastic? What problems does one face with transplanted organs? How does the practice of transplanting and re-attaching body parts compare with Mary Shelley's conception of Frankenstein's monster?

•Someone from another planet. Compare life there to here.

•A future cook. What's left to cook? What new foods have been developed?

•A married couple on their 300th wedding anniversary, deciding whether or not to renew their marriage contract. What's it like being married to the same person for centuries? What are the new alternatives to marriage? What physical, social, political, and economic changes have occurred?

•A computer.

•The devil, on the future of evil.

•God, on the future of religion.

•A person who can read other people's minds.

•A clone. Do clones have feelings? How do they feel about the originals?

•The sanitation man or woman of the future. How is waste disposed of? Is anything recycled? What did we do in the 20th century that created problems in the 21st?

•A robot.

•A future postal service employee.

•A CIA agent in the future.

•Generations of the same family.

•Figures from the past whose views of the future altered history.

•People who predict the future (prophets, clairvoyants, weather forecasters).

•An artificial life form.

•A future urban dweller.

•A future policeman.

•A person who was "frozen" and just revived. Would he or she want to be refrozen to wake up in another future? How long would "frozen people" want to experience the present world before suspending themselves again? How far ahead in the future do they want to be revived?

• The mayor of a future city. What forms of energy are used? Where does the water supply come from? What is the educational system like? How did city planners plan for recreation? What kind of housing is available? Public services?

• The mayor of Utopia City—the perfect city of the future.

• Plan a debate between candidates during a presidential election. What are their campaign promises? What stands do they take on contemporary issues of the future?

• Members of radical political groups, and anarchists of the future.

• A representative of Appalachia discussing the influence of that culture on the rest of America, and the establishment of the state of Appalachia.

• Members of a committee to draft a new Constitution.

• Members of a committee to draft a constitution for a commune.

Notes

1. Alvin Toffler, ed., *Learning for Tomorrow* (New York: Vintage Books, 1974), p. 3.
2. Billy Rojas, "Futuristics, Games, and Educational Change," in *Learning for Tomorrow,* p. 219.
3. Ibid., p. 220.
4. Michael A. McDanield, "Tomorrow's Curriculum Today," in *Learning for Tomorrow*, p. 105.

8

Loose Tubes . . .
Interpersonal Communication on Video

A human being is not a black box with one orifice for emitting a chunk of stuff called *communication* and another for receiving it. And, at the same time, communication is not simply the sum of the bits of information which pass between two people in a given period of time.[1]

Ray Birdwhistell

Elements of Communication

At its simplest, communication involves transporting messages through time and space, in symbolic form, from source to receiver. Messages can be disrupted at any point by the introduction of "noise" (problems in decoding or encoding information), resulting in misinterpretation. Communication is also affected by the *relationship* between the sender and receiver. An aspect of human behavior is socialization, and it is impossible for human beings not to interact—even silence is a form of communication.

The symbols exchanged between senders and receivers are usually words, but body and voice are media as well. Movements and gestures form a nonverbal language developed from birth which replaces, negates and reinforces words. Yet, as an affective (rather than "intellectual") area of education, it is generally discriminated against in educational institutions.

Video recording is a "natural" for humanistic and confluent education. It is a means of bridging the gap between linear, logical and verbal aspects of cognitive learning (functions of the left hemisphere of the brain); and the intuitive, holistic and nonverbal aspects of affective learning (the neglected functions of the right hemisphere). In its starring role as Orifice of the Living Room, TV only emits, but in its role as classroom *communicator* it enables us to see, analyze and change ourselves in both the cognitive and affective domains. One form of noise that can distort messages is the projection of our own personal experiences and feelings. With the VTR, students have the unique advantage of being able to observe their "video selves"—to refer back to their behavior as actually recorded, and to be independent of someone else's noise for feedback. As Harold Lyon states,

> ...I am not suggesting...that teachers should practice therapy in the classroom. Clearly, the classroom is not the place to dig deeply into an individual's past. Educators, however, have been too shy in dealing with "here and now" feelings which invariably foment between students, and between students and teachers....What I am advocating is that they have the courage to push forward—and push hard—against the boundaries that are keeping them confined purely within the cognitive realm. They must widen their sphere of influence to include the affective domain as well. Only by stepping out and taking the inherent risks—risks which are present in all meaningful human encounters—will progress be made.[2]

Exercises that enable students to see themselves as others see them, to realize their positive and negative values within a supportive atmosphere, to heighten awareness of internalized emotions and to understand how their actions affect others, should not present problems beyond the teacher's control. Aids to help students answer "Who am I?" and "Does anyone else feel the way I do?" are valuable in every classroom, for every subject. Activities that leave students with negative, unresolved or unchanneled observations should be avoided and are best left to trained therapists.

This chapter focuses on nonverbal communication and role playing. The exercises are useful as video games and acting projects; for generating scenes and story ideas; for developing physical and vocal expression, positive self-images and social interaction on the elementary level; for providing guidance and personal feedback on the high school level; for communication arts, sociology and anthropology courses on the university level; and as a diagnostic tool at any level. Video tape influences behavior. Once observed by the subject, body language can be controlled, miscommunications corrected, and students' understanding of one another heightened.

In order for communication exercises to be effective, the teacher too must be willing to share feelings and experiences. Depending upon the purpose of the exercise, students tape one another or the teacher photographs the class. Preferably, both should occur. (It is difficult to trust a person who is not willing to participate in the process himself.) It is possible to explore relationships from the standpoint of literature, psychology (e.g., how people relate in small groups), and the social sciences (e.g., territoriality—how people set aside specific areas for their use). The activities might be a visual log of students' interactions throughout the year.

Nonverbal Communication

> When a facilitator creates, even to a modest degree, a classroom climate characterized by all that he can achieve of realness, prizing, and empathy; when he trusts the

constructive tendency of the individual and the group; then he discovers that he has inaugurated an educational revolution....Learning becomes life, and a very vital life at that.[3]

Carl Rogers

Learning about the self and others involves real-life experiences. The following activities allow for physical and emotional expression and build trust, cooperation and a positive sense of community through the sharing of feelings and ideas. They create a "climate" for affective and cognitive education.

Interpersonal relations: activities

Sculptor

Use pairs. 'B' assumes a relaxed, neutral position standing or lying on the floor. 'A' molds 'B' into different positions, rolling and bending parts as if working with clay. Reverse roles. Sculptors should concentrate on working slowly and carefully (not forcing the model into unnatural or painful positions), becoming aware of the variety of movements possible. Models should try to relax completely and trust their partners, observe their success or failure at this on tape, and observe how the positions they were placed in compared with positions they felt they were in.

Slow motion fight

Partners engage in a slow motion fight, without using physical contact. Slow motion fighting requires cooperation and control, and is a positive outlet for aggressive behavior. Be certain a real give-and-take situation has occurred. During playback, emphasize that every action requires a reaction; every thrust a rebound. Stage a slow motion fight as part of a dramatic production.

Organism

Small group. Students join together by holding wrists and proceed to explore the environment as a single organism. Any part of the organism can take the lead at any time. Play back, observe and discuss struggles for leadership, how they were resolved, and how it felt losing individuality to the group. Was it ever pleasurable to conform to the group movement? When in real life does conforming become a necessity? Social studies students can analyze how group decisions are made; discuss the positive values of compromising and giving up individuality to solve a common problem. Discuss the negative aspects of "blind conformity."

Masks

Entire group (or small groups) seated in a circle. The first person transforms his or her face into a mask (a fixed expression), looks at the student next to him who mirrors (exactly copies) the mask, turns and faces the next person while changing into a new mask, and so on around the circle. Art students might want to "freeze" the frame (stop the picture), sketch, and perhaps make actual masks.

Haiku

After performing several sensory exercises, students in language arts classes can transfer their feelings into words in the form of *haiku* poetry. The poetry can then be taped as short scenes combining narration (reading the haiku), movement (interpreting the imagery of the poem), sound (using sounds abstracted from the words themselves)[4] and projections (painted or transparent images cast on a screen or on the actors from an overhead projector).

Inner-outer

Pairs. Students improvise a given situation such as "first date" or "job interview," saying one thing but communicating just the opposite through body movement. Document several improvisations on tape, select the best moments from each and use as the basis for a scripted scene.

Nonverbal messages may be communicated intentionally or unintentionally. People use them to manipulate a situation or may simply be communicating real emotions they feel but cannot, for a variety of personal or situational reasons, express. In *Mastering Classroom Communication,* Dorothy Hennings lists several clues that indicate a conflict:

a. a slight hesitation that indicates a speaker is less than enthusiastic about doing something.
b. signs of irritation, anger, fear, unhappiness masked behind a calm exterior—shaking hands, blushing, tightening of the lips, heavy swallowing
c. gestures and facial expressions that contradict the spoken message
d. tensions of the muscles that conflict with a calm tone of voice
e. an abrupt change—an initial reaction covered up immediately[5]

Follow-up and related activities. Try to find examples of inner-outer behavior expressed by politicians, interviewers and guests on television. Using a variety of materials (paper, objects, photographs), create a box representing your public self on the outside, and your inner (private) self on the inside. In small groups, try to determine who created each box. Produce two brief abstract video tapes, one showing your inner self, the other, your outer self.

Dictionary of feelings

Entire group. Students come up individually in front of the group to demonstrate a gesture we would immediately associate with a specific emotional state or feeling. (You might want to evolve a list of emotions first.) The rest of the class tries to identify the emotion and suggest alternate means of expression. Try to evolve a gestural vocabulary—physical positions everyone would agree represent the corresponding emotional states. Tape the vocabulary and play it for another class, e.g., one in communications arts or cultural anthropology, with the sound and narration off, to see if the vocabulary is understood.

Research and follow-up activities. Is it realistic to establish such a vocabulary? Can you think of any instances where stock gestures would be useful, even necessary? Do people always respond in the same way to different situations? Compare *your* dictionary to the "laws of expression" and "science of applied aesthetics" of Delsarte,[6] the stock characters of the commedia dell'arte, the development of stylized dance, and the techniques of pantomime artists. Explore how physical positions are used in art to communicate a message.[7]

Explore nonverbal communication in films and on television—especially in silent films and the mime of Chaplin.[8] Find examples of body movement in conflict with itself or with verbal expression. Watch television with the sound off, especially game and talk shows, and observe nonverbal messages communicated through gestures, facial and eye expressions, large body motions and posture. Turn the picture off and listen for verbal and vocal stimuli that express feelings; listen for what verbal stimuli can tell you about the speaker's educational background, social background, feelings about the topic and the role the speaker is playing.

Personal space: activities

We all have personal spacial "bubbles" we protect or allow other people to enter. Edward T. Hall describes four specific boundaries we project from our bodies: intimate space (up to 18 inches), personal distance (18 inches to 4 feet), social distance (4 feet to 12 feet), and public distance (over 12 feet).[9]

Do you agree with these invisible boundaries? Who do we generally allow into each of these spaces and how do we prevent people from entering? What happens when someone enters a space uninvited? Do personal spaces affect the way we move, feel and communicate during our daily interactions with others?

1. Look for places (libraries, buses, school cafeterias) where you can record and subsequently examine the way people deal with overcrowding. Where are strangers more likely to tolerate spacial invasions? In front? To the side? What nonverbal reactions can you identify?

2. Record instances where you or several students deliberately enter a person's space, gradually moving closer and closer. Observe and discuss the subject's response. This can be especially valuable in an *un*crowded environment ... but be certain to move in by degrees, and explain to the "victim" afterwards what was happening.

3. Role play and tape an interrogation.[10] What kind of environment would you choose for an interrogation? What kind of lighting and props? How can spacially "assaulting" a prisoner aid the interrogators? What did it feel like being interrogated? After viewing, discuss evidence of nonverbal expressions and how the scene could be made more compelling through camera techniques.

4. Improvise short scenes on how the manipulation of space can affect relationships between people.

Environments: activities

Environmental psychologists claim that physical settings condition our ability to work or play, our search for or avoidance of other people, and our preferences for various activities.[11]

The Elevator Exercise

Mark a square on the floor with masking tape to serve as an "elevator." Ask students to enter the square one at a time, until the area is filled to capacity. As space bubbles shrink, what do people do with their bodies? Do they appear relaxed? Uncomfortable? Excited? Protective of their spacial territory? Ask participants how they feel, before playing the tape. Does the playback confirm what they said?

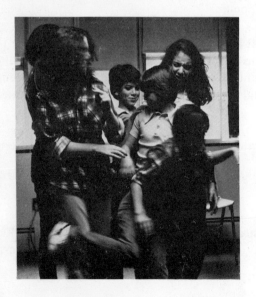

Any part of the environment (kitchen, work space, housing, museum, sports arena) can be manipulated to heighten or decrease the effects on their inhabitants.

1. Tape a variety of home and public environments (including other schools) and discuss them with the rest of the class. Which seem most pleasing, stimulating, calming and inviting, or isolating or frightening? How does the organization of a room become a form of personal expression? Does the seating arrangement imply any form of hierarchy? Is there any indication of distance control? Does everyone respond similarly or are there several responses to each environment? Tape an interview with a community planner or architect.

2. Do a tape focusing on beards. Interview their owners: Why did they grow them initially? Why do they keep them? How do they groom them? How many different styles can you identify? What do they want to communicate, and what do you *feel* they communicate? Try a montage of beards with appropriate music and/or sounds. Find the earliest and longest example of a beard you can. How do styles differ from culture to culture, and throughout history? When were beards "in" and "out," and why? What have been their various associations (beatniks, artists, biblical references...)?

Role-Playing

Role-playing, according to Shaftel and Shaftel,[12] is a group problem-solving method that enables students to spontaneously explore, discuss and evaluate their behavior. Video tape further enables them to view themselves objectively and refer back to their action. Like future studies (see Chapter 7), role-playing involves students directly in the process of decision making, helps them sort out environmental overload and counter the effects of one-directional black boxes, clarifies basic values within particular cultures and subcultures, and encourages ethical behavior within those cultures. When used in conjunction with nonverbal, humanistic and other improvisational exercises, students learn to become sensitive to and respect individual differences; to see (behavioral) alternatives; to resolve conflicts; to understand that the way they behave causes certain reactions; to express and manage their feelings; and to learn social behavior with the support of other students. Taping and playing short scenes in special education settings releases tension and develops positive concepts, skills and acceptance. Older students have the opportunity to determine individual and group values.

Readers interested in the theory and technique of role-playing, and those not already convinced of the importance of spontaneous play in education, will find Shaftel and Shaftel's *Role-Playing for Social Values* informative. The role-play topics below (Table 8.1) encourage thought about different life-styles and situations.

TABLE 8.1: Role-Play Situations

• typical parent behavior (situations that explore father/mother roles or the way parents are portrayed on TV)
• typical adult behavior
• typical child behavior
• typical teacher or principal behavior
• situations where you feel victimized

- putting others down; getting yourself put down
- conformity and being controlled
- being excluded from a group
- feeling lost
- attitudes toward work and leisure
- roles in government
- individual integrity—honesty, responsibility for others
- manipulative roles: pacifying, avoiding, blaming, preaching
- scenes involving affective relationships: friends, enemies, lovers, family
- scenes involving behavioral relationships: dominant/submissive, exhibitionist/spectator, dependence/nurturance

Suggested formats for role-play

1. Record improvised role-playing situations in the areas listed in Table 8.1. Students then discuss and analyze what they said and did and how their behavior affected others in the dramatization.

2. Use role *reversal* for solving real conflicts (demonstrations, rejections by a group, student protest). If possible, the actual people involved should participate.

3. Dramatize an incident involving a conflict and the making of a moral decision. Play the tape and stop it at the decisive point. Students discuss and act out in class how the situation should be resolved. Or tape and present several possible solutions for students to choose from. Half the class might produce tapes for the other half. Students might develop situations for younger students or other classes.

4. Working in small groups of five or six students, present problem situations. Each group writes its own dialogue and tapes the scene; tapes are subsequently shown to and discussed with the entire class.

5. Role-playing situations can be developed from literature, films, plays and historic incidents as well as real-life situations. For example:

- courage, cowardice, and war (*The Red Badge of Courage*)

- something you would like to but cannot do; parents living through their children; lack of communication; meeting or not meeting expectations; individualism (*Death of a Salesman*)

- rituals, groupings, conflict and power; fear, pride and pretense; taunting for differences; causes of violence (*Lord of the Flies*)

Notes

1. Ray L. Birdwhistell,*Kinesics and Context* (Philadelphia: University of Pennsylvania Press, 1970), p. 3.
2. Harold C. Lyon, Jr., *Learning to Feel—Feeling to Learn* (Columbus, OH: Charles E. Merrill, 1971), pp. 80-81.
3. Carl Rogers, in *Learning to Feel—Feeling to Learn,* p. 85.
4. Activities on using language for musical purposes can be found in Don Kaplan, "The Joys of Noise: Part One," *Music Educators Journal* 62 (February 1976): 36-44.

5. Dorothy Grant Hennings, *Mastering Classroom Communication: What Interaction Analysis Tells the Teacher* (Pacific Palisades, CA: Goodyear, 1975), p. 36.

6. See Ted Shawn, *Every Little Movement* (New York: Dance Horizon, 1954).

7. See John P. Spiegel and Pavel Machotka, *Messages of the Body* (New York: Macmillan, 1974), Part Two.

8. "When Charlie Chaplin portrayed the Tramp in 'The Gold Rush,' he mimed a delicious meal—a feast—using as the culinary high-point an old boiled shoe. Starved and frozen to near numbness in the wilds of Alaska, he and his somewhat disbelieving partner gorged on shoe laces, filet of leather sole, and shoe nails as succulent bones. In transforming a cooked boot into nutriment, he banished hunger and pain and put fantasy and entertainment in their place. The act of renunciation and the denial of painful reality were perceived by the audience as both pathethic and delightful, bordering on madness but with a saving grace: Reality was delicately transformed through the minutely constructed operations of make-believe.

These qualities—magical beauty, pathos, absurdity bordering on insanity, and fun—are the special transformations the Mime imposes on messages it transmits...."

Spiegel and Machotka, *Messages of the Body*, p. 47.

9. Edward T. Hall, *The Hidden Dimension* (Garden City, NY: Doubleday, 1966), pp. 110-120.

10. "Spacial invasions are not uncommon during police interrogations. One police textbook recommends that the interrogator should sit close to the suspect, with no table or desk between them, since 'an obstruction of any sort affords the subject a certain degree of relief and confidence not otherwise obtainable.' At the beginning of the session, the officer's chair may be two or three feet away, 'but after the interrogation is under way the interrogator should move his chair in closer so that ultimately one of the subject's knees is just about in between the interrogator's two knees.' " Robert Sommer, *Personal Space* (Englewood Cliffs, NJ: Prentice-Hall, 1969) p. 28.

11. See, for example, Albert Mehrabian, *Public Places and Private Spaces: The Psychology of Work, Play, and Living Environments* (New York: Basic Books, 1976).

12. Fannie R. Shaftel and George Shaftel, *Role-Playing for Social Values: Decision-Making in the Social Studies* (Englewood Cliffs, NJ: Prentice-Hall, 1967), p. 9.

9

Skewed Pictures. . .
Video Journalism

The first thing that the photographer learned was that photography dealt with the
actual; he had not only to accept this fact, but to treasure it.... But he also learned that
the factuality of his pictures ... was a different thing than the reality itself.... The subject
and the picture were not the same thing, although they would afterwards seem so....
The photographer's picture was not conceived but selected....[1]

John Szarkowski

You know, a picture doesn't lie. I know that and you know that. That is why television
is such an enormously effective medium. But while a picture doesn't lie, a picture may
not tell all the truth.[2]

Richard M. Nixon

The most difficult thing to come by in television is the truth. Documentaries are intended to
be representational (showing real-life situations as they actually occur) but they often present
a subjective, rather than objective, point of view. The news is supposed to be "the honest and
unbiased and complete account of events of interest and concern to the public,"[3] but the same
"actuality" will appear differently on each channel. One station will emphasize calm speeches
during a veterans' holiday, another, militant overtones. A recent coup in Thailand was treated
differently by each country that covered it even though footage came from the same source.
Japan provided its own background and light relief; the U.S. played down the event; the BBC
claimed students were "ardent;" the Dutch were not sure students were armed; South Africans
were sure they were armed, The Germans saw students as victorious, and Hungary placed a
greater emphasis on the political background.[4]

Realities are determined by those who are recording and looking at them. Every production step involves a choice—which way the camera will point, which parts of a scene will be framed, what time of day to shoot—creating predetermined, stereotypical or new visions. The following section heightens students' awareness of the "realistic" representation of the world through electronic journalism, enabling them to arrive at their own conclusions concerning the actualities on television and to control the actualities *they* present in the classroom.

Electronic Journalism

A whole new breed of TV comedy-variety show has evolved. It is the local newscast.[5]

Staging the news

Radio signals make the news immediately accessible over short distances to large audiences, or between two or three people. There are no cameras to set up, many news reports during the day (allowing greater scheduling flexibility), and a greater emphasis on local news since stations operate within city limits. Since reports occur often during the day and night, more "late-breaking" stories can be presented with frequent updates. The range of reports offered is increased since there is no necessity to choose only visually interesting material.

The use of portable *video* equipment has, of course, made events more accessible, but television still has to limit its coverage to stories that are visually exciting. A story with film usually takes precedence over one that must be read from the anchor desk. If there is film, the action film will almost always replace the film that includes only a conversation or discussion (talking head). Genuine intelligent discussion is not "good" television.

During a fixed length of 22 minutes (after commercials and station announcements), all the daily news—whether stretched or condensed—must be presented.

> The result is that some informal, unacknowledged laws of television news have developed: unattractive faces are almost never on camera in "good guy" roles; a fire at night will almost always be shown though an equally serious daytime fire won't; every news story must be complete within one minute and fifteen seconds, unless the program is doing an "in-depth" treatment, in which case one minute and forty-five seconds may be permitted. All this has led to an overriding law—The Trivial Will Always Drive Out the Serious.[6]

The news is still part of television. And all television programs have to compete.

> It is a perfect example of the dilemma of news producers. They want to present the news, they want to keep it in perspective, but they are also a part of television, an entertainment medium depending at all times—including during news broadcasts—on attracting the largest possible audience to deliver to an advertiser. Since news is part of an entertainment medium, it must be entertaining.
> And a peaceful bus ride [re: the busing issue] is simply not entertaining. What *is* entertaining is a shrieking confrontation between blacks and whites, preferably with the shiny helmets of the National Guard for additional "color" and the threat of serious violence.[7]

The news is unintentionally distorted by producers' efforts to gain high ratings. Delivering the truth is difficult under normal circumstances; it becomes almost impossible when the news is deliberately controlled to promote a particular viewpoint.   Radio news evolved from print journalism, and television, while similar in style to radio journalism, has to balance audio and visual elements. The absence of visual images on radio requires the listener to imagine what a person or event looks like—a quality often lamented with the invention of television. This lack of visual information helped less-than-charismatic politicians achieve prominence; a charismatic appearance on television has become a necessity for the successful contemporary politician. Not only people who make the news, but people who deliver the news, gain prominence by appearing on television.

Copywriting: structure, subjects and verbs

Since information is heard only once, it must be understood the first time. Short, declarative sentences "energize" a story. When producing video journalism, avoid complex dependent and independent clauses and inverted sentence structures. Active verbs (which describe rather than merely report occurrences), contractions, and close subject/verb placement will improve flow, add clarity, and provide a sense of immediacy to the broadcast. Avoid clichés and mixed metaphors; use repetition (with reason) for reinforcement, and "write as you talk." Material that reads well on paper may not communicate well when heard. Read everything *aloud* to eliminate clutter, increase drive and comprehension. Delete any word or sentence that does not help communicate the information. Use personal pronouns to provide an intimate quality.

Placement of the subject within a sentence prepared for broadcasting is different from its placement in a newspaper or magazine story. Names get attention. In print the reader sees a name, wants to know more about that person and is "hooked." A well-known name can be used as a television news lead, but other names have to be cued—preceded by a descriptive phrase preparing the audience. Subject identification (title, age, job) also precedes the name, unless the sentence becomes unclear. If unfamiliar initials are used, precede or follow them with the full name. Titles should be simple, retaining the most important information.

The source of a statement or story should be identified (with editorials clearly indicated) when the statement is controversial, to establish credibility, or when it is an integral part of the story. Attribution should not be made without reason. Short quotations (or longer ones broken up by naming the source) need a distinct beginning and end, but do not need to be identified by the words "quote" and "unquote" (e.g., the principal's "exact words were"; the mayor "said" or "called").

Electronic journalism is instant news. A paper has to state whether the action occurred today or yesterday; a broadcast does not have to state the word "today," except to clarify information. The immediacy of the medium allows television to update stories as they unfold by including new information, causes and motives not part of previous broadcasts. A daily news program produced by students can update an event occurring inside or outside the school by following the story as it develops each day, interviewing the school population for its reactions, projecting how the event may affect the audience and offering editorial comments. Newspapers follow the familiar inverted pryamid style, telling the most important facts first and other information in descending order of importance. However, in radio and television news a narrative style following the lead is more natural. Broadcast leads do not include the five Ws (who, what, where, when, and why) since too much information is presented too quickly.

Leads (on video) include important information that attracts the viewer and prepares him for what follows. (An "umbrella" lead implies that a number of related stories is about to be presented.) Statistics should follow the lead to be certain they are not missed, and common story elements can be used as transitions to provide continuity. A short sentence or sentence fragment acts as a headline and tells the listener what to expect. If the news is presented daily, students might want to try an additional format, the "mini-documentary" (a serialized report, each segment usually three-and-a-half minutes long, with a separate introduction and conclusion). Broadcasts should include national and international as well as local school and community news. This will require students to locate stories in several sources, encourage them to compare their coverage to that of commercial television, and stimulate interest in reading newspapers. Seventy-five percent of Americans get most of their news from television; 50% get *all* their news from television.[8]

Manipulating the news

> Research into audience preferences in New York and Los Angeles has revealed that newscasters who could reduce the anxiety level of audiences and present the news in a context of reassurance, had tremendous appeal.[9]
>
> *Robert MacNeil*

> We're in the boredom-killing business—we'll tell you any lies you want to hear.[10]
>
> *Paddy Chayefsky*

In *The Gods of Antenna*, Bruce Herschensohn, formerly Deputy Special Assistant to President Nixon, states that "without conscience, President Nixon had created a Boredom Crisis within the United States..."[11] and supports his thesis by describing techniques used to deliberately distort the news. According to Herschensohn, we lost the Vietnam war because of slanted media coverage working against our involvement. Journalistic devices were used against Nixon and our allies in Southeast Asia, CBS was used by Hanoi as a propaganda outlet, and reality was intentionally distorted by the media. Watergate was pursued because of a period of boredom between the reelection of Nixon and the fall of South Vietnam.

Herschensohn's list of distortion techniques includes applications of methods already mentioned and several other subliminal practices at the broadcaster's disposal:

●Story placement. Increasing or decreasing the significance of a story by grouping and order (e.g., the lead story is the most important); implying associations by moving from one story to another without pausing or using a narrative bridge.

●Stop action. Giving the (psychological) impression of allowing us to see something we missed or shouldn't have seen, leaving us with a moment that may have no significance at all.

●Editing. Giving the appearance of a smooth transition while actually relieving the conversation of some carefully chosen words, or substituting a different answer for the question given.

•Focal length. Changing the apparent size of a crowd to minimize or expand support for a given issue.

•Crowd reaction. Omitting or including reactions to the advantage or disadvantage of the subject.

•Leaving out visuals. For example, talking about "spacious quarters" when the visual would prove just the opposite.

•Crediting or discrediting through choice of words. "The *stated* purpose of the investigation ..." implies it was not the *real* purpose.

•Acting. Emphasizing particular words or phrases; reading slowly or quickly.

•Nonverbal communication. Nods, grimances, faint smiles and assorted gestures used to editorialize; posture and placement of commentator used to communicate authority or kinship with the audience.

•Opinion. We are impressed by the "facts" when opinions are being given without acknowledgement (facilitated by the transient nature of television).

•Half-truths. Intentionally giving the wrong impression by leaving out information.

•Catch phrases. Using editorialized phrases that become part of the national vocabulary and can be directed against a subject—"antiwar" (implies those opposed to it are "prowar") and "The Saturday Night Massacre."

•Guilt by association. Showing one thing and saying another; making a statement and following it with a visual that appears to support it but really doesn't (again facilitated by the transient nature of television).

•Graphic emphasis. Spoken words can be emphasized by showing them to the viewer on the screen, adding editorialized importance to phrases that maybe insignificant or taken out of context.

•Pretense. All sides appear to be represented, but the report is biased—accomplished by adding material that didn't occur that day or with that event, or endorsing or opposing a candidate by giving more negative background elements for one than for the other.

•Resurrection. Reviving interest in a non-news story; adding an old story out of context, or as if it had a relationship to current events.

•Killing a story. Ignoring follow-up stories when they oppose the chosen viewpoint.

•Creating news. Sustaining a continuing story by interviewing people about "The Story," talking about what wasn't talked about, or talking about the fact that there is no new news about the story.

Activities

Try the following exercises to explore the journalistic process in class, and to understand the processes affecting what we see and hear on commercial television.

1) What is "news"? What differentiates news from history? Write news bulletins for historic events; write a list of current news publications that a student reporter should read.

2) Tape the news off the air as broadcast on the major networks. What reasons can be provided for discrepancies between reports? Which channel is most manipulative? Most objective? What is the news "format"? How do televised reports compare to newspaper treatments of the same events? Write a profile of a particular newscaster.

3) Produce a newscast following the usual format (as observed above), including the news, weather, sports, advertisements, editorials, patter and humor, reviews, consumer affairs, and credits. Assign journalistic roles (differentiating between newscasters and news commentators), decide what is newsworthy, gather stories, and determine which stories should appear, what order they will appear in, and how long they will be. Include at least one "media event"—a "happening" created to give the journalist something to cover (e.g., interviewing and following the principal around the school without a definite purpose, intention, or issue to be addressed). Use a variety of journalistic approaches and styles (intellectual, sarcastic, confrontational, emotive, detached).

4) Cover an event that will also be covered by broadcasters. Compare reports. Follow-up on a news story you feel was inadequately handled.

5) Tape a satirical newscast using pseudo news, emotive techniques, humorous attitudes toward tragic occurrences, and any other theatrical techniques you can exaggerate that make the news the comedy-variety show it is today.

Notes

1. John Szarkowski, "The Photographer's Eye," in *Mass Media and the Popular Arts,* ed. Frederic Rissover and David C. Birch (New York: McGraw-Hill, 1972), pp. 313-315.

2. Richard M. Nixon, cited in *Coping with Television,* ed. Joseph Fletcher Littell (Evanston, IL: McDougal, Littell and Company, 1973), p. 113.

3. Duane Bradley, cited in *Mass Media and the Popular Arts,* p. 95.

4. From the broadcast, "World: The Clouded Window," WGBH-TV, produced and directed by David Kuhn.

5. *Time,* as cited in *Coping with Television,* p. 94.

6. Frank Mankiewicz and Joel Swerdlow, *Remote Control: Television and the Manipulation of American Life* (New York: Ballantine Books, 1978), p. 97-98.

7. Ibid., pp. 91-92.

8. Ibid., p. 94.

9. Robert MacNeil, cited in *Coping with Television,* p. 95.

10. Paddy Chayefsy, "Network."

11. Bruce Herschensohn, *The Gods of Antenna* (New Rochelle, NY: Arlington House, 1976), p. 72.

10

Open Circuits . . .
Interviews and Documentaries

We live in the age of the Information Explosion. Every day, our senses are bombarded by information stimuli: Buy this product; vote that way; conform to the standard; be aware; expand your consciousness! In such a time, everyone ought to become a journalist, in the truest sense of the word, for the journalist is one who looks beyond events and examines their significance. Henry David Thoreau kept journals detailing not only minute observations of nature but also their significance in the large scheme of things. When he described a battle of ants at his doorstep, he also was writing of the wars that have plagued mankind since the beginning of history. There is Stephen Crane, talking about the human element in the Spanish-American War. There is Edward R. Murrow, conquering time and space to make the Battle of Britain a part of our lives, and leading the electronic crusade against McCarthyism. There is the participatory journalism of Ernest Hemingway and George Plimpton, the kind of journalism that gives the amateur a chance to relate to the exploits of another amateur engaged in the world of, say, the professional bullfighter or football player. Who among us has not had the dream of deep-sea fishing or pitching an inning against the New York Yankees? Journalists sometimes bring out the Walter Mitty in all of us.[1]

Chuck Anderson

Tapes are not merely documents. They show how human beings are alike and different, examine systems, tell about individuals, families, communities and their roots, and how the past influences the future. The process of video documentation develops skills in conducting research, note-taking, collecting and organizing information, creating questionnaires and attitude surveys, arriving at generalizations based on the analysis of data, and presenting results in a comprehensible fashion. It heightens interest in print materials and encourages personal expression and informed editorial statement. Knowing more deeply about one another builds trust. Sharing experiences encourages new friendships and stimulates communication, listening and language development.

It is useful to know the rules of journalistic interviewing and documenting before starting but rules should be approached with caution. Get involved in the process first. Be as objective as possible. The techniques will become necessities after the production has begun; before it, they may serve only as obstacles to be overcome.

Preparation

The primary responsibility of a journalist to the public is to obtain information. Determine the subject and purpose; research and investigate thoroughly. It is important to know what the issues are, in order to ask probing questions. Choose a suitable environment in which to tape. A natural environment lends credibility, but don't interfere with regular traffic or transactions (e.g., blocking entrances to stores or buildings). Decide whether interviewer/ subject interaction is necessary—should the interviewer be seen during the interview?

Several arrangements may need to be made prior to interviewing or documenting. School regulations need to be ascertained, approval from authorities at the chosen site and any other necessary arrangements secured. Try to visit the site first. Find out as much information as possible so it can be used to best advantage. Arrange for transportation, permits, finances, and food as necessary; assign crew responsibilities (one person on camera, one on VTR, the interviewer on microphone, and one person to act as technical director and "advance person" to set up the interview). Prepare questions, and decide who will be interviewed. (Choose people who are part of the group you want to represent.) Follow visits with a thank you note. It is courteous and necessary if you ever want to be invited back.

Depending upon the format and journalistic approach being used, production plans may include a storyboard. Check the indoor environment for outlets, excessive room noise, light, and other possible technical problems; outdoors, watch for visual distractions, wind noise and other audio problems. A certain amount of ambient noise contributes to the realistic quality of a tape as long as it doesn't interfere. Watch for light reflection and battery failure. In both instances try out different camera angles and shots. (See Tables 10.1 and 10.2). Careful preparation will result in a relaxed and organized taping session.

Interviewing

Interviewing skills can be developed by practice. Some helpful techniques:

•Use a hand-held camera whenever possible for realism. Hold microphones six to eight inches from the mouth. Preferably, keep the microphone in an intermediate position rather than switching it back and forth.

•Establish credentials. Identify who you are, what organization you represent, the purpose of the interview, and what will be done with the tape.

TABLE 10.1: Directing an Interview

- Standard positioning: All subjects are on one side of the interviewer.

- One-shot: For a series of short, impressionistic answers to a stated question (the interviewer is never seen). Use a bust shot or close-up.

- Two-shot: Open on a two-shot of subject and interviewer; zoom in slightly and pan to favor the subject (or eliminate interviewer completely). Either person can be favored during the interview (zooming in for intensity), moving the camera where the viewer would look if he or she was present. Zoom out to close with a two-shot. One person can do an interview by taping himself with the subject and editing out entrances and exits, or by staying behind the camera and using the built-in microphone.

- Over-the-shoulder shot: Described previously, used here to create an intimate feeling.

- Walking shot: Follow the subject and interviewer using a mid-shot, keeping the camera as steady as possible, and avoiding cables.

- Cutaway: Used to show something happening near the interview, to show crowd reaction or (in an over-the-shoulder shot) to show the interviewer listening to the subject. When a single camera is used an interview is taped from start to finish, opening with the interviewer alone or in a two-shot, then recording the subject's responses in their entirety. Afterwards the interviewer is taped "listening" and cut into the subject's responses.

- Crowds: Be prepared to zoom out to a bystander who suddenly voices an opinion; for spontaneous conversation; and for more opinions as the crowd gathers.

TABLE 10.2: Directing a Panel Discussion

Format:

- Establish setting and panel (titles can be supered over the scene).

- Zoom in to moderator for introduction.

- Pan to each member of the panel as he or she are introduced (in order).

- Cut to moderator for the question.

- Cut or pan back and forth between panel members and moderator during the discussion (zoom in for intensity).

- Cut to moderator for summary.

- Zoom out to re-establish scene.

Evaluation:

• Were shots, visuals, audio and video elements used to advantage and of good quality?

• What contributed to the quality of the discussion? Was the subject well chosen?

• Were the speakers prepared? Did they present facts or opinions?

• Did a single speaker monopolize discussion? Did speakers talk to each other or to the camera? Which, in this format, is preferable? How did nonverbal cues contribute to the conversation?

• How skilled was the moderator in keeping the conversation on track? Did he or she monopolize the discussion? Direct the conversation in a productive manner? Allow participants to answer questions? Summarize periodically?

• Were shots, visuals, audio and video elements used to advantage and of good quality?

• Modify panel techniques for small group discussions (without a moderator).

• Relax the subject. Evoke interest with a gentle lead question. Maintain eye contact at the same level. If the subject is seated, the interviewer should be seated; if the subject is active, join the activity. Be aware of personal space. Sit or stand at a distance comfortable for the subject and the camera. For a prepared interview, shoot a test sequence so the subject can see and hear himself. Engage him in light conversation before the interview (but not on issues concerning the interview so that the interview itself will be "spontaneous"). Tell the subject what the questions will be, about the intended audience, and why he or she was chosen to be interviewed.

• Focus questions on the "here and now." Use questions the subject can identify with from his or her own experience ("How do you *feel* about...?"). State the premise ("Con Edison claims there is nothing they can do about exploding manhole covers ... that it's an act of God."); ask the question ("Do you agree that nothing can be done about covers exploding under your feet?"), and expand into additional questions based upon the response.[2]

• Be patient, honest and respect privacy. Be aware that some people approach the media with hostility and suspicion (with some justification!).

• Provide opportunities for rephrasing (e.g., for "yes" and "no" answers). Emphasize and elaborate, but don't dominate the interview. Keep the viewing audience in mind.

• Don't repeat answers. It slows down an interview and appears as if the interviewer is stalling for time while thinking of the next questions.

• Listen and show real interest. Do not enter with preconceptions that may not conform to the actual situation. Avoid thinking about the next question instead of the answer; let the answer lead you to additional questions.

●Photograph subjects and aspects of the scene to which the interviewee refers. In a walking interview, questions can be stimulated by moving through the environment.

●Wrap up (summarize) at the end of the interview.

●Express gratitude to subjects for their participation. Replay the interview through the in-camera monitor if desired; get written permission to use the tape.

●Follow up by replaying tapes, abstracting and writing main ideas, and combining interview results with questionnaires to form generalizations.

●Edit to eliminate distractions and repeated answers, and to shorten pauses. (Prepare for editing by making a list of everything on the tape including time, shot and whether or not the footage will be used.)[3]

Avoid the common manipulative techniques of creating an attitude, prompting, speech writing and inappropriate attire. Don't create an unbalanced interview. See Table 10.3 for a description of "video verité."

Interview resources

●Interview handicapped people. Talk about fears, feelings, problems of coping with handicaps, alternate ways of living.

●Investigate winners and losers. What makes a person a winner? A loser? Which characteristics of winning and losing do you possess? How have people transformed themselves from losers into winners?

●Survey attitudes toward clothing, hair, social relations and life-styles. Design questions that require interviewees to evaluate people based on incomplete information. What do responses reveal about prejudices? Using a hidden camera, document people's reactions to the same person dressed in different ways.

●Interview members of the faculty and administration on school issues.

●Speak with elderly and other people who spend their time watching television. How does television reassure them and substitute for human interaction?

●What sex roles and family stereotypes do people assume? Who should do the dishes? Who should make household repairs?

●Interview authors, composers, videomakers and other artists in their studios and/or homes. Include examples of their work, explore their lives, and discuss opposing attitudes toward their work.

●Interview people who have read a controversial new book, If possible, interview the author and discuss the results of your previous interviews.

• Talk with people who have lived through major historic events.

• Interview students from other countries.

• Choose a problem found in an advice column and ask people what advice they would give.

• Interview yourself. Prepare questions, tape yourself asking them, tape yourself answering them and giving your opinions, tape yourself reacting. Then assemble the interview.

TABLE 10.3: Video Verité

Video verité is the purest form of video anthropology. A "true" documentary, it is intended to capture certain aspects of reality without manipulation or preconceptions; the process of the event is the basic focus of the recording.

• Approach the subject unobtrusively. "Disappear" from the scene; don't disrupt or intervene in the process you are recording.

• Maintain an attitude of exploration and discovery. Be ready for anything.

• Do *not* use a script or formally prepared questions. Informal research into the subject is an advantage, but avoid preconceptions.

• Avoid the use of actors, although individuals can agree to portray themselves while interacting with the event.

• Have enough equipment to be prepared, but not to be overburdened.

• The smaller the crew, the greater the likelihood of recording the event accurately.

• Let the tempo and rhythm of the event direct your pace and prescribe the shots. Keep pace with the action.

• Edit as objectively as possible. Assemble rather than restructure the event. Avoid voice-overs or imposed sound effects.

• Results are intended to be spontaneous and real. Poor lighting, sound, and occasional lapses of focus are acceptable.

• Play back tapes for their participants, obtain permission and record participants' feedback on the tape.

Source: Adapted from Yvonne Elisabeth Chotzen, "Videotape Verité in the Study Process: A Methodology for the Porta Pak VTR," *Audiovisual Instruction,* March 1977.

Documentary resources

The school as a resource

The school provides many situations for video documentation:

• Arriving at school for the first time. Interview new students, re-enact experiences and discuss doubts and fears.

• Using school facilities (library, guidance center, gymnasium); recording aspects of school life.

• Improving scheduling techniques. Document changes from class to class and cafeteria operations to improve mobility.

• Identifying potential safety hazards.

• Recording reports for presentation to the Board of Education or Superintendent; presenting reports from the Board or Superintendent at faculty meetings (tapes shared within the entire district).

• Taping instructional games and simulations.

• Sponsoring and documenting a television in-service workshop for teachers; documenting teachers' centers' activities, special services programs.

• Visiting other schools and examining alternative modes of education.

• Recording a discussion on student rights.

• Producing a satirical tape on teachers, students and schools as institutions.

The community as a resource

Use what your community offers:

• Taking field trips to zoos and aquariums (how animals are cared for, general maintenance, sources of funding, jobs), botanical gardens, monuments, factories.

• Reporting on hospitals, day care centers, mental health agencies and senior citizen homes. What facilities are available? How do the people in these institutions feel about them? How do institution personnel feel about the people?

• Exploring and recording visual pollution (litter, discarded automobiles, unauthorized

VIDEO INTERVIEWS sharpen the skills of the student journalist and foster communication among students. Note the position of the interviewer (to one side of the two interviewees), the upstage hand holding the microphone, and the low angle of the shot.

dumping, billboards and commercial signs). What can you tell from trash? How much does your family produce? What is the trash situation like in your neighborhood? How is it disposed of? Investigate a junkyard.

• Exploring local history. What can a cemetery reveal about the history of your community? What do names of streets, local architecture and historic sites reveal about your town's heritage?

• Discovering grass roots history. All people are walking anthologies of stories, poems, and rhymes. Prserve the oral tradition by collecting stories, real and imagined incidents, and folk tales. Collect and demonstrate dying arts, ethnic recipes and reminiscences from rural areas. Incorporate interviews, still photographs, and audio recordings into the final tape on the history, heritage, life and unique culture of a region (like the *Foxfire* project on Appalachia).[4]

• Documenting community events, such as parades, kite flying contests, street festivals, political occurrences.

• Producing a series on local government for use within the school district.

• Taping both sides of a community dispute. Explore how the problem arose, create a dialogue, and investigate solutions.

Nature as a resource

The world of nature, too, provides endless areas for video documentation. Some ideas are:

• Exploring the impact of man on nature. How have uninhabitable regions become habitable? How has the construction of a new road or water system contributed to the development of your own community?

• Creating a series of tapes to prepare for natural and man-made disasters. Identify types and cause/effect patterns.

• Reporting on man's relationship with animals—from evolution to extinction.

• Investigating air, water, and solid waste pollution.

• Reporting on energy conservation methods.

What else can be documented?

Video, like our eyes and our words, can delineate the issues and processes of contemporary life. It can detail such varied areas as consumer awareness, movements of popular psychology, cable and public access television, support for the arts, and thanatology.[5] Video can investigate crime and punishment, apathy, violence, civil liberties, genetic disease. None are simple topics, but video is a tool for their understanding.

Notes

1. Chuck Anderson, *The Electric Journalist* (New York: Praeger, 1973), pp. 78-79.

2. Even this simple question is not objective. The choice of the word "exploding" adds drama to the question, and the question is phrased in a manner that causes the subject to identify with the action involved ("under *your* feet?").

3. More specific information on editing (from more than one tape with an editing deck) can be found in Don Harwood's *Video as a Second Language: How to Make a Video Documentary* (New York: VTR Publishing Co., 1975).

4. *Foxfire* is a student-run magazine dedicated to the collection and preservation of the oral history, folklore and folklife of Appalachian Georgia.

5. See Elisabeth Kübler-Ross, *Death: The Final Stage of Growth* (Englewood Cliffs, NJ: Prentice-Hall, 1975).

11

The Inner Tube...
Programming and Advertising

TV has been attacking us all our lives, now we can attack it back.[1]

Nam June Paik

You keep thinking you should have been reading, or something.... Fat chance. Television viewing, like nailbiting, is something you will stop tomorrow.[2]

Paul Klein

Recall, for a moment, returning home as a child and being confronted with "What did you learn in school today?" The inquisitive parent asked the same question every day and probably received the same response: "Nothing."

We are always learning—from ourselves, from others, from the media environment—even if we are not always aware of it. What is "learned today" comes from a variety of sources and is both consciously and unconsciously acquired. It may include facts, physical skills, trivia, incorrect information, good or bad habits, attitudes, values or emotional responses ... and a primary source of learning is the television.

In the make-believe world of television commercials, we learn that dusting every day will help us pass the white glove test; that pure Corinthian leather is infinitely more desirable than plastic; that the "funny blue stuff" will keep us brushing longer, make our teeth brighter, and assure our success in dating. But do we think about the implications of the nosy menace who invades our homes looking for a speck of dust or what we spend paying for the privilege of sitting on leather upholstery in a gas-consuming car?

If future studies help students control their lives from the inside-out, studying the "inner tube" helps them understand what controls their lives from the outside-in. Television manipulation is subtle ... we see only the players, not their real motives. Advertisers employ sophisticated techniques to convince us that their product is biggest and best and basic. News and entertainment programming set moral, social and economic standards. This kind of information is absorbed for more hours than the average student spends in school. The viewer is learning by experiencing, but the experience is passive—there is no participation, opportunity for questions, interaction or feedback. By using video tape in the classroom, those affected earliest by these messages can understand inside school today what television is telling them to do outside school tomorrow.

Programming's Impact on Society

> In the past twenty years, television has become a powerful intruder in the traditional processes by which parents and teachers impart values to children. It is a dangerous intruder because it portrays excessive violence, gives children a silly picture of adult life, encourages a deadly passivity, and creates a fantasy world in which entertainment is the highest value and every problem is readily solved.[3]

> *Frank Mankiewicz* and *Joel Swerdlow*

It is possible to explore television's "manipulation" through taped interviews, documentaries, panel discussions, video reports or dramatizations.

The American image

How does television portray doctors, detectives, soldiers, teachers, radicals, lawyers and priests? What was the last thing you saw on television that made you proud to be an American? Think about how social class is generally portrayed, and how this might affect poorer classes of people who are unable to attain a particular life-style. What is the potential buying power of the poor and what effect does this have on advertisements? How often does television show the best, rather than the worst, of minority and ethnic life? Discuss and document how male and female sexual images are promoted. What characteristics can you identify? Identify instances where sex is treated realistically (demonstrating authentic sexual maturity) and as a fantasy (the playgirl/ playboy image). Tape your own version of the Miss America contest.

Investigate how soap operas contribute to the American image.

> The "soaps" on television are a national institution. Each week day, without fail, they are attended by over 20 million people, far more than attend many of our better recognized and catalogued institutions....
> As with all established institutions, soap opera teaches and demands certain values, foremost among which is loyalty. The prime sin, to a soap opera viewer, is to Miss an Episode, and as a result millions of lives are regulated by whether *Love of Life* appears before or after *As the World Turns*.[4]

> *Frank Mankiewicz* and *Joel Swerdlow*

"Soaps" differ from other dramatic programs in the portrayal of time, subject matter,

Commercials

Advertisers spend great amounts of money and use a sophisticated combination of psychology and showmanship. Commercials appeal to our "creativity" (add your own ingredients to the packaged formula) and to our desire for power, control, security (a well-stocked refrigerator) and sense of worth. They relate to our responsibility to the family and need for love objects. Advertisers know you don't want to be left out (everybody's doing it) and you certainly deserve it (whatever "it" is); they'll play on your snob appeal, say it's patriotic and, above all, will make you more youthful. "Take it from me—it's new and improved, it's exclusively ours. And here are your neighbors to endorse it."

Viewers are likely to find messages delivered to them straight ("May I have a few words with you about ... diarrhea?"), as dramatizations, demonstrations, or through personifications (the Scrubbing Bubbles, Chiquita Banana).

Advertising techniques

The most common selling techniques include:

• The bandwagon. Don't feel left out ... nine out of 10 do, so why don't you? Music, symbols or movement will be used to show you what you're missing.

• The testimonial. A well-known person—preferably a hero—endorses the product.

• Transference. Something people feel good about is transferred onto the product. Symbols (the flag) are often used to transfer feelings.

• Plain folks. Confidence in the product is achieved by the viewers' identification with the common man—the "roots" technique.

• Snob appeal. Directed toward our desire for status.

• The glittering generality. Catchy slogans, words and general terms are used without definition or specific qualifications.

• Name-calling. This is a judgment of the competition ("smoother than," "better than") without evidence.

• Buzz words. Popular, positive words are used to describe a product (e.g., "pure" or "natural").

• Slogans. Easily mastered by the consumer to help him identify and remember the product.

• Loaded words. Contain a high emotional appeal, but can also be misleading. "Family recipe" conjures up images of mother stirring the pot.

• Card stacking. Half-truths, past truths, untruths; deception through simplification and making more of something than it is.

●Hidden fears. Ads that attack our insecurities (Will *you* be the one to find a bottle of mouthwash in your desk drawer?).

●Repetition. "New Lemon Wash-It-All has a lemony-fresh scent and comes in a lemon-yellow bottle. Just look for the lemons on the label on your grocer's shelf..."

●The direct order. The commercial tells you what to do ("Go buy it now!"), appealing to our need for authority.

●Facts and figures. Used to "prove" a point ("Five out of six doctors recommend..." but over *what*?).

●Time and money savers. Statements suggesting the price is lower than the competition's, that this product will save you money or time.

●Persuasion. Incorporating classic elements of persuasion: ethos (building confidence in the character of the persuader), logos (appealing to the mind or reason) and pathos (appealing to emotions, desires and needs). The elements may be genuine, but can also be deceptive, outright false or appeal to less honorable desires such as greed, lust and conquest.

Student activities

Produce television commercials in the classroom. Draw a storyboard first, being certain to apply visual continuity and pacing techniques. Ads can be created for real or invented products, to sell a movie, book or article, to promote the school, or to stimulate tourism in the community or state. Local television stations will often provide 16mm commercials they are no longer using for student study.

Videotaping ads is another cross-disciplinary activity that involves students in a number of areas. Non-English-speaking students can write commercials in their own language, try to translate one into English or produce ads without dialogue; English-speaking students can translate foreign soundtracks or dub soundtracks into a language they are studying. Food commercials should be studied in terms of nutrition (what good or poor habits are being taught), selling techniques, product quality and budgeting. Career education, language arts, theater, music, art, social studies and media classes can all benefit by producing commercials and focusing on their particular areas. Specific exercises might include the following:

●Conduct market research. Interview people in the supermarket, asking why they are buying a particular product. Have they ever bought a product they saw advertised on television? Were they satisfied? Does age, sex or occupation determine who will buy what?

●Invent a product, package it, write a slogan and jingle. Tape two or three treatments of the same commercial, then choose the one you feel is most effective and show it to the class. Would viewers actually buy this product? Why? Of all the products students present, which names are most remembered a few weeks later? Which products are recalled by their slogans or jingles? Analyze the results, and redesign the product and/or commercial as necessary.

• Many ads will conform to the establishing shot/mid-shots and close-ups/reestablishing sequence. Since advertisers have only a few seconds in which to sell their products, this pattern provides a way to tell the "story" and convey the message in a concise and dramatic manner. See, for example, the following script for a commercial. After studying it, write a script for a different product.

TABLE 11.1: Script for a Commercial

VIDEO	AUDIO
SHOT #	
1. FADE IN LONG SHOT of restaurant interior. DAISY (the waitress) is behind the counter, drinking a cup of coffee. JOE and MARY enter.	MUSIC: UP. "Mood" music on radio.
2. THREE SHOT of DAISY, JOE and MARY. JOE and MARY sit down at the counter.	MUSIC: DOWN AND UNDER.
	JOE
	(Excitedly.) I still can't believe it! A landslide victory! Daisy, meet the new Deputy Mayor!(He knocks over the cup of coffee.)
	MARY
	(Horrified and embarrassed.) What a mess! Let me help you.
	DAISY
	(Matter-of-factly.) Don't worry. I have all I need right here.
DAISY reaches behind the counter and pulls out a roll of "Supraspongey" brand paper towels. ZOOM IN to CU and TILT DOWN to counter top.	JOE
	That will never do the job.
	DAISY
	Just you watch!
DAISY pulls out a second brand of towels (the competition), two glasses filled with tomato juice, and proceeds to perform the absorbancy test, dipping first "Supraspongey" brand paper towels, then the competitor. She squeezes both towels over the counter showing that, indeed, "Supraspongey" has absorbed more tomato juice.	DAISY
	Now, here's a roll of *your* paper towels. Look at how much faster new "Supraspongey" absorbs that juice!
3. CU of JOE.	JOE
	(Pleasantly surprised.) Oh!
4. CU of MARY	MARY
	(Absolutely amazed.) Ahhhh!

5. THREE SHOT of DAISY, JOE and MARY. DAISY is standing, arms folded, with an "I told you so expres—sion on her face. DOLLY BACK to LONG SHOT and JOE and MARY exit, leaving DAISY to clean up spilled coffee, tomato juice, broken cup, etc.

MARY
Let's pick up two rolls of "Supraspongey" now. I'll need one for around the house, and one for the office.

6. CU of "Supraspongey" brand paper towels.

MUSIC: UP. "Supraspongey" jingle from the radio.

• Decide on products that would best be served by the preceding format; write, then produce the ads on tape.

• Create a storyboard for a commercial seen on television.

• Compare the number of shots in several 30-second commercials. How often does the camera viewpoint change? (The number of shots may vary from one to 20 or 30 in a single ad.)

• Produce counter-commercials. Choose ones you feel are offensive, misleading or dull; identify what you feel should be changed, and redo them. Discuss which ads are in "good" and which are in "poor" taste, and whether good or bad taste determines if people actually buy the product. Which ads are most interesting? Which are the worst? Why?[8]

• While the visual message is generally clear without the sound (turn down the volume and observe for yourself), audio is still an important element. A total absence of sound can even be used as an attention-getting device. Produce a purely visual commercial, explore a variety of soundtracks for a new ad, add a track to someone else's tape, or dub in a new soundtrack for an old one.

• Produce the ads of the future. Which products will still appear on the screen? What new ones will be introduced?

• Produce public service announcements, based on community needs, and ads for school organizations. Create ads promoting products that are good for children (e.g., vegetables). Analyze the success of the ads by showing them to children in a neighboring school and interviewing them afterwards for their reactions.

• Have your own Clio awards ceremony for the best ads.

• Identify the "average" American image by watching commercials. Which ads use female voiceovers, and which use male? Do male or female voices dominate? How are men or women discriminated against in ads?

• Create ads that make really dull, everyday products sound exciting.

• Analyze the language of advertising (paragraph structure, length of sentences, use of abstract or concrete words). Compare television commercials to magazine and newspaper

AFTER TAPING A VIDEO COMMERCIAL, students analyze the results. Producing their own tapes makes students more alert to the manipulative techniques of commercial advertising.

advertisements (comparing the same product, if possible). What are the verbal and visual differences?

•Report to the Federal Communications Commission local broadcasters who remove parts of programs (monologues, credits, interviews) in order to sell more ads.

•Can ads be considered "art" (i.e., can they evoke the same kind of emotional and intellectual responses associated with pure art)? Should ads be abolished?

Notes

1. Nam June Paik, as quoted in Gene Youngblood, *Expanded Cinema* (New York: E.P. Dutton, 1970), p. 302.
2. Paul Klein, "The Men Who Run TV Know Us Better Than You Think," in *TV Action Book* Evanston, IL: McDougal, Littell and Company, 1974), p. 96.
3. Frank Mankiewicz and Joel Swerdlow, *Remote Control* (New York: Ballantine Books, 1978), p. 256.
4. Ibid., p. 207.
5. Ibid., p. 56.
6. Edith Efron in *Remote Control*, p. 19.
7. Frederic Rissover and David C. Birch, *Mass Media and the Popular Arts* (New York: McGraw-Hill, 1972), p. 4.
8. "Some television commercials are actually applauded by viewers. In Rome, Italy, for example, television commercials for an evening broadcast all appear in one nightly half-hour slot. It is listed in the television schedules as 'La Caricalla.' If you happen to be in Rome when 'La Caricalla' is on, get out of the way of youngsters and adults who will literally run you down to get to the television set. Millions view 'La Caricalla' nightly ... and if you ever see it ... you'll know why. Each commercial is a complete 2 to 4 minute story complete with characters, plot, conflict and climax...." Don Hessler, "Using Television Commercials in the Classroom," Los Angeles Unified School District Instructional Planning Division, KLCS-Channel 58. (n.d. Mimeographed.)

APPENDIX A

VERTICAL HOLD: VIDEO ART

Pure video art explores the medium for its graphic potential rather than for its ability to communicate audiovisual information, using the tube as a source of light rather than a surface reflecting light. Approximately 7½ million individual phosphorescent dots are on the face of a screen per second. Combined with television's ability to control and manipulate spectrum colors, the video artist, according to Gene Youngblood, has a "a fabulously rich mantra of color, sound and motion" with which to work—an "electronic experience unlike anything the cinema has ever known."[1]

Video graphics are regularly shown in museums, libraries and galleries as "exhibit" tapes. While schools owning a basic black and white portapak have only one "pure" videographic technique available (the video feedback described below), additional techniques become accessible with the use of multiple cameras and a special effects generator.[2] Using video tape as an expressive medium is not limited to the "swirling diaphanous lines and clouds of light, crumbling faces and ghostly superimpositions"[3] of pure video art—it can include any form of personal or private expression.

By synthesizing some familiar techniques, students can create new ways of using *video as an art form:*

•Experiment with oddly juxtaposed subjects, shadows, unusually framed shots, and canted shots. Explore subjects (objects or people) by photographing them from a variety of unusual angles, distances and levels.

•Create an abstract tape by floating subjects against a black background (a person dressed in black with white gloves and white face).

•Choreograph dances for the medium. Be certain the dancer(s) can be seen on the small screen; remember to work in depth rather than width, and do not frame the dancer so that he or she unintentionally goes beyond the parameters of the screen. A spotlight or backlights can be used to separate the subject from the background; a shallow stage photographed with a long lens can increase stage depth, but will also deepen faces and bodies (this may be used to advantage). Experiment with incorporating the subject into the background (the dancer becomes part of a kinetic backdrop), using graphics projected against a white backdrop or projected on the dancer.

•Tape natural and man-made geometric patterns, textures, and architectural forms in the environment. Look for objects and activities that normally escape our awareness.

•Tape microscopic organisms and add a soundtrack (see Chapter 6); dramatize two amoebas having a conversation; place the camera on an animation stand and tape abstract patterns created by splattering colored oil in water.

•Try to communicate odor, taste and touch through aural and visual means.

•Visualize poetry and secret wishes. Tape a video autobiography.

•Use bits and pieces of visuals and sounds to create abstract images; show the entire subject (as a whole) at the end.

•Create a video collage by presenting many different shots in a short period of time (the shots can be thematically related, or composed of video "graffiti"—unrelated shots).

•Experiment with video feedback. Connect the VTR to a receiver via the RF adapter,[4] adjust the zoom lens and f-stop, point the camera at the receiver, and observe the "visual echo" (the image will repeat itself continually, with each repetition smaller than the last). Vary light and controls on the camera and receiver; turn the camera and/or the monitor; zoom in and out; combine visuals with poetry or music; shoot through fingers or goboes (camera shields) to create abstract images.

•Find something beautiful and tape it.

Notes

1. Gene Youngblood, *Expanded Cinema* (New York: E.P. Dutton, 1970), p. 295.
2. With a nonportable VTR, switchers and special effects equipment, techniques such as the following become available: polarity reversals (negative images), sweep reversals (mirror images), wipes (pushing one image off by another in different patterns), inserts (one image inserted into another), the "joy stick" (moving particular effects into different parts of the screen), split screens (combining two pictures separated by a horizontal, vertical or diagonal line), multiple-source split screens (splitting the screen into several pictures), keying (adding information, e.g., a title, with the new image covering and blocking out part of the old image), chroma keying (using specific colors to process portions of the background picture electronically), debeaming (creating high-contrast images), and colorization (adding colors to black and white pictures, creating abstract patterns).
3. Gene Youngblood, *Expanded Cinema,* p. 295.
4. A monitor can be attached directly via the video input on a nonportable VTR.

APPENDIX B

STAY TUNED: LISTENING SKILLS

In a painting, every part can be seen at once within a two-dimensional frame. In music, one has to wait to experience the entire composition. Sounds have a cumulative effect. Each note, phrase, sequence, group of sounds or movement is dependent upon what precedes and follows it, building gradually as the total composition reveals itself. In order to use sounds effectively in time/space media, students need to develop their *aural literacy* ... to isolate, sort out and control the "aural surround" for the effective communication of sound.

Little, if any, attention is given in schools to developing listening skills, yet these same skills are essential for functioning in the world, for heightening concentration and for developing the ability to follow directions. To listen well means to analyze and efficiently use aural information, to listen in context and to identify main ideas and supportive details. Any exercise that heightens students' awareness of aural images, their combinations and their potential applications will lead to more informed producers and more creative soundtracks.

Working on the Skill

• Ring a bell, play a single note on an instrument, or make a resonant, noninstrumental sound. Ask students to close their eyes and concentrate on the number of vibrations they can hear after the initial attack. Produce the sound again, and have students focus on how long it takes for the sound to completely fade. Do it a third time and ask students to visualize the shape of the sound and any colors that they might associate with it.

• Working in pairs, students *simultaneously* relate an incident or tell each other what they have done so far that day. They should speak continuously and not stop to listen but rather attempt to listen while they are talking. After a minute or two, on a signal from another person, they stop and alternately tell their partners what the *partner* said.

•Choose a simple, familiar tune such as "Three Blind Mice" and ask each student, in turn, to sing one word of the song, maintaining correct rhythm and melody. Repeat the exercise several times until it sounds as if one person is singing.

•With a partner, students decide upon a single nonverbal sound they can perform in unison. After physically separating themselves, the students close their eyes, begin walking and making their sounds, and use "selective listening" to rejoin their partners.

•Students close their eyes and walk slowly while humming a tone in unison. The teacher or director touches a student on the shoulder; the student hums a different tone, and, as they become aware of the change, the other students adjust to a new unison on that pitch. Repeat several times, working toward more rapid adjustments and increased ability to discriminate smaller changes.

•Record commonplace sounds on audio tape. Play back, and ask other students to identify the "mystery" sounds. Turnstiles, electric mixers, and roller skates may all become unrecognizable when removed from their visual associations.

•In a group, tell a story through sounds, and then tape it. Can the rest of the class determine what the story is? Create an environment using only sounds.

Perspective, Association and Context

Just as an establishing shot orients us visually, sound can be used to familiarize the viewer with a scene, establish a setting or prepare the audience for what follows. We expect images to sound in particular ways. What sounds do you associate with a zoo? A tiled bathroom? A city street? When the sound does not match the image, the aural/visual relationship becomes odd or amusing. The effective communication of sound for realistic aural/visual relationships depends upon physical projection (intensity based upon origin, distance, and the angle) and matching the quality of that projection to the quality of the visual image. A flat sound emanating from a baseball field lacks depth and will seem unnatural for that location. Excessive ambient sound during an intimate scene will be obtrusive, destroying the quality of the scene. "If we know what an audience expects, we can fulfill or disrupt its expectations on purpose, for a purpose."[1] "Light" the subject with sound; heighten students' awareness of perspective, acoustics and aural/visual relationships by using the following exercises.

•Ask students to choose at random a number, word, name or meaningless sound (the sound is only needed to facilitate the exercise). Each student, on his or her own and remaining in a stationary position, directs the sound toward the floor so that it reaches the floor but stops there. He attempts to project the sound so that it covers the distance needed to arrive at the ceiling, but no further; and then directs the sound to each of the four walls. Project the sound toward different objects at different locations in the room.

•Students move to random positions in the room. Without altering position or turning his head, one student sends a sound to another student in the room. The entire class points to the person it thinks the sound has been directed toward; the sender either confirms the response or tries again. (By asking the class to point, the student can visually determine the direction of sound perceived by the group.)

•Using a meaningless sound, students walk up to different objects and surfaces (this may include other people) and project the sound against or into them, observing the effect each substance has on the quality of sound.

•On audio tape, record aural equivalents to long shots, close-ups and mid shots.

•Produce a video tape on *un*expected aural/visual relationships—loud sounds from frail subjects, objects projecting human sounds, body parts moving to machine sounds, mouths speaking music rather than words (synchronized to instruments of the orchestra). Try using the hidden camera approach to document the reactions of people encountering sounds for which they were not visually prepared. Analysis sould focus on why we expect certain objects or images to sound in particular ways, and can be extended into discussions concerning other expectations (stereotypes, roles, life-styles).

•Our perception of sounds is also dependent upon their context. Ask the class to pass a sheet of ordinary notebook paper from person to person, absolutely silently. Was silence achieved? What sounds did the class hear? How noisy did the sounds appear to be? Were there grimaces when a fingernail tap, finger slide, rub or ripple occurred? While we generally ignore such commonplace sounds, they can be considered "noisy" when removed from their usual context, or when used within a particular sequence. If a paper passed between two people was preceded by sirens and followed by cannon fire, a rustle would hardly be noticed; if placed between a modest hiccup and a slight sniffle (increasing our concentration and attention), a fingernail tap becomes dramatic. One sound can overwhelm and force us to withdraw; another inhabits a small aural space in a large area of sound, drawing us toward it in an intimate manner.

•On audio tape, experiment with timbre (quality), pitch, volume, duration and harmony, using instrumental, vocal, electronic, verbal and concrete (found sound) sources to produce various aural effects.[2] Tape TV programs off the air and add new soundtracks; use an abstract soundtrack as a basis for creating video visuals. Tape a crowded room where everyone shouts at one another or speaks inaudibly. (Are there any visual clues to explain their behavior?) Explore associations with whispers (e.g., intimacy and secrecy) and apply them, where appropriate, to your productions. Would whispers be as effective on film? Use rhythm to achieve emotional effects; to contrast and to support visuals; to heighten the viewer's awareness of sounds through repetition (forcing the audience to hear peripheral sounds); and to focus attention on the absence of sound through the disruption of a repeated pattern.

Manipulation

Music and sound effects can be used to elicit specific behavioral reactions. The most familiar examples of this technique are the "uh, oh" organ chord (the unwed mother returns to ruin the family name), the "watch out!" crescendo (at the moment of suspense) and the "chuckling plunkets" (played by the strings, accompanying the comic interlude). The sounds themselves help to produce the desired audience response (dismay, alarm, amusement). The same effects can be accomplished on a deeper, more effective level through more subtle uses of auditory stimuli such as conflict expressed by pulsating or grating percussive sounds or suspense by silence.

•Record sounds to express specific emotions. (Can the class agree on how emotions should sound?) Play the tapes for another class to find out how effectively the emotions are communicated.

•Recall instances, chosen from television and film, where you were especially moved. Do you remember what sounds accompanied the images? Ponderous live themes and horrifying effects often become amusing. Less obvious soundtracks have more impact.

•Compile a list of musical clichés, then use them for satires and soap operas.

Notes

1. Tony Schwartz, *The Responsive Chord* (New York: Anchor Press/Doubleday, 1973), p. 33.
2. Exercises in vocal, verbal and found sound sources can be found in Don Kaplan, "The Joys of Noise: Parts I and II," *Music Educators Journal* 62 (February and March 1976).

APPENDIX C

THE CANDID ANTHROPOLOGIST: BODY COMMUNICATIONS ON VIDEO

The Smile

Bodies, as an expressive medium, are incredibly complex. A single movement such as extending the corners of the mouth or pulling the upper lip upward can communicate a snarl, a grimace or a smile. The expression of a smile varies from country to country; it can be genuine or false, and can represent humility or grief, hostility or embarrassment, as well as pleasure. Even a baby's smile might be ambivalent, natural or threatening.

•Look up the definition of "smile"; demonstrate and record each meaning in class. Can you agree on one expression that communicates kindliness? Diabolical intentions?

•Find examples of smiles in art. What do they communicate to you? Why are these people smiling?

•Become a cultural anthropologist and produce a tape on smiles. Record people who are smiling, ask others to smile, or tell a joke. Add an appropriate soundtrack. How do the smiles differ?

•Write the word "smile" so that it looks like its meaning; invent a new word for "smile" that sounds more like its meaning.

•Write a dramatic scene starting with "What are you smiling about?"

•To heighten awareness of *facial* communication, produce a tape with narration and accompanying action satirizing the various facial movements available, their possible combinations, and meanings: brow behavior (lifted brow, lowered brows, knit brow, single brow); lid closure (overopen, slit, closed, squeezed); nose (wrinkle-nose, compressed nostrils, bilateral nostril flare, unilateral nostril flare or closure); mouth (compressed lips, protruded

131

lips, retracted lips, apically withdrawn lips, snarl, lax open mouth, mouth overopen); anterior chin thrust, lateral chin thrust; puffed cheeks, sucked cheeks.[1] Try demonstrating positions individually, showing several combinations and explaining their "proper" use (in a positive or negative manner) with other people. Refer to Birdwhistell's "Face Kineograph"[2] for a list, with appropriate symbols, of facial expressions.

The Communicative Hand

Hands, like smiles, can be used as a basis for interdisciplinary video studies incorporating nonverbal communication, documentation and dramatization. You might try the following exercises:

• Using eye contact only, find a partner. Facing each other, place your palms against each other and close your eyes. Do *not* attempt to communicate anything—simply experience the contact. After several moments, nonverbally decide to part hands, open your eyes and move on to another partner.

• With a partner, close your eyes and have a nonverbal conversation with your hands. Say hello, exchange some feelings, · have and resolve a conflict, say goodbye. Tape the conversations and ask others what they saw communicated.

• Have your palm read. Tape an interview with a palm reader; tape a lesson on palm reading.

• Research the origin of the word "hand" and produce a documentary on the origin of hand gestures and their meanings in various cultures and within the same culture. (Suggestions: victory/peace signs, thumbing a ride, gestures in sports, religious and meditative gestures.) Research the evolution of the human hand.

• Evolve as many variations of the handshake as you can, giving each a different meaning or emotional content. Express one thing verbally and communicate another through your handshake; develop handshakes that invite people in and throw people out the door. Demonstrate the handshakes on tape, and incorporate them into dramatic scenes.

• Show "The Hand"—a Czech film using puppet animation—as a lead-in to discussions on domination, power, politics and totalitarianism.[3]

• Develop a multidisciplinary unit on another aspect of nonverbal communication—the foot, wink, walk or bow.

Notes

1. Ray L. Birdwhistell, *Kinesics and Context: Essays on Body Motion Communication* (Philadelphia: University of Pennsylvania Press, 1970), pp. 100-101.
2. Ibid., p. 260.
3. "The Hand" (by Jiri Trnka, 19 minutes, color); available from Contemporary/McGraw-Hill Films, 1221 Avenue of the Americas, New York, NY 10020.

APPENDIX D

FEEDBACK: USING VIDEO TO MEASURE TEACHER PERFORMANCE

Observing a lesson on video tape not only reveals a teacher's personal style and effectiveness, but helps identify student behavior the teacher may not have been aware of while involved in the educational process. "Noise" (messages transmitted in conflict with those that were intended) and effective or ineffective classroom management skills can be seen objectively; general and special educational needs can be diagnosed by analyzing nonverbal behavior and social interaction. Taping lessons facilitates unbiased evaluation and enables the teacher to review his or her behavior several times for analysis. Student as well as teacher performance can be verified and discussed. By observing actual performance in the classroom and how one person's behavior affects another, the viewer defines educational goals more clearly and makes better choices for achieving those goals.

Decide what you want to observe, record the discussion or activity and use the guide below (Table D.1) for feedback.

TABLE D.1: Checklist for Teacher Performance

• What do you like about yourself? Which techniques have you seen other teachers use that you are using effectively or have improved upon?

• Which role or combination of roles do you play as teacher? The law (completely authoritarian)? Facilitator? Resource person and guide? Best friend?

• How involved are students in the activities you plan? Can you identify changes in facial or body expression that indicate attention gain or loss? Are discussions teacher or student centered? Do they wander? Do certain students monopolize the discussion? How can you lead other students into participating? Are students encouraged to respect different viewpoints? Is the lesson supported by facts rather than biases? Do you handle discussions fairly and in a supportive manner? Does the discussion have a conclusion, and are learning goals achieved?

• Can everyone see and hear? If mobility is necessary, are students able to move about freely?

• Do you elicit questions? Rephrase questions and answers to emphasize them? Are you satisfied with yes/no answers or do you encourage students to elaborate? Do you accept other solutions to problems or only the ones you expected? Interrupt answers or allow other students to interrupt answers? Do you build student comments into the discussion? Use sarcasm against students? Do students always direct their answers toward you or share them with other members of the class?

• Do you communicate anything that tells children they cannot be trusted? Are they given opportunities to participate in areas of decision-making where they can assume responsibility for their actions?

• How do you resolve conflicts? Do you center conflicts around yourself?

• Do you have any distracting verbal or physical habits? How do you interact spacially with students? To what extent do you use body language? How expressive are your face and eyes and what do they communicate? Are your nonverbal messages ever in conflict with your verbal ones? Do you use them to reinforce, emphasize and clarify what you are saying?

• Which physical positions characterize your teaching style? Do you communicate interest through body posture? Are you physically overdramatic or inhibited? How do you focus students' attention? Can you identify any verbal/gestural combinations? How do you acknowledge participants? Can you find examples of "hidden" prejudices toward an activity or student in your nonverbal behavior? What messages does your clothing communicate?

• Is your speaking voice monotonous or does it vary in pitch? Is it too loud or soft? Do you speak too quickly or slowly? Are your words, body and voice all sending the same message?

• Do you vary your sentence patterns? Are the length and complexity of your sentences and your choice of words appropriate to the level you are addressing? Are you using nonstandard forms or dialects? Is your speaking style formal or impersonal?

• What new abilities have you discovered by viewing yourself? What would you like to change?

The following publications will be helpful for teachers interested in additional feedback resources:

Theodore W. Parsons, *Guided Self-Analysis System for Professional Development Education Series* (2140 Shattuck Ave., Berkeley, CA, 1971.) It includes worksheets for video tape analysis.

Theodore W. Parsons, William Tikunoff and Patricia H. Cabrera, *Achieving Classroom Communication Through Self Analysis* (Studio City, CA: Prismatica International, Inc., 1973).

Sue Hawkins, "Tape Record Your Teaching: A Step-by-Step Approach," *Learning Resources* Vol. 2 No. 2, April 1975.

APPENDIX E

DUE TO CIRCUMSTANCES WITHIN OUR CONTROL:
TROUBLESHOOTING AND VIDEO TAPE CARE

The best use of video equipment requires careful purchasing, planning for preventive and corrective maintenance, and efficient scheduling for students and teachers. When purchasing equipment consult an expert (e.g., the school media technician), select a reputable company, and choose those systems or units that will *actually* be used and are compatible with your needs. Tapes, transistors and microcircuitry are sensitive to such changes in the environment as temperature, humidity and dust. An appropriate storage space is one which protects the equipment, is accessible to teachers and students, and is secure against damage or theft. It will have working space for maintenance and the capacity for expansion, will protect tapes and equipment now and prevent disappointments and costly delays in time and money later. As the demand for the equipment increases, breakdowns will also increase. Budget for repairs and replacements; make arrangements with the school media technician; or locate a nearby shop that will provide fast and efficient service.

Specific information on the care of video tape (Table E.1), its general maintenance (Table E.2) and "troubleshooting" (Table E.3) follow.

TABLE E.1: Do's and Don'ts of Video Tape Care

• Do not use computer tape instead of video tape.

• Some tapes have oxide problems. Record a few minutes of a new tape, and check the playback for dirt and clogging. (If they appear, return the tape.) Be certain to watch the playback from the tape, not from the live monitor (which bypasses the tape).

• Avoid extremes in temperature. Allow the VTR to warm up slowly in cold weather, and allow the tape to reach room temperature before using it.

• Avoid touching tape with the fingers.

• Do not use tape near chalk or smoke.

• Thread the tape carefully to avoid scratching, tearing and stretching.

• Lifting and squeezing the hub can damage the tape edges; lift the hub by the lower flange only.

• Do not drop or bump into the reels (the reel flanges may bend, causing improper feed).

• Allow reels to coast to a stop after playing or rewinding. Stretching can occur if the reels are pressed down manually.

• Be certain the tape pack is smooth. Check the transports for too much or too little tension.

• Removing tape in the middle of the reel can cause permanent damage.

• Never stop tape in mid-reel without releasing the tape tension. Read the directions and use the *standby* and *still frame* buttons carefully, being certain the tension is released.

• Cut off wrinkled ends. Damaged tape can cause misalignment, ruin the entire reel and damage the video heads. If wrinkled tape in the middle of the reel is straightened out, work on the dull side or even more iron oxide will be lost. (The shiny side has the oxide.)

• Use the proper tape for splicing and splice on the dull side.

• Use only the recommended tape to secure tape ends.

• Do not write on the end-of-tape stickers when they are on the reel; several layers of tape can be dented.

• Keep tape ends off dirty surfaces, and leave enough leader so that damaged ends can be cut off.

• Label tapes carefully for future reference.

• Store tapes away from magnetic fields.

• Store tapes vertically in their original boxes, and return tapes to their boxes immediately after use.

• Store tapes under moderate temperature and humidity conditions.

• For long-term storage, rewind the tape from end to end to assure uniform tension.

TABLE E.2: General Maintenance Tips

• Clean the heads and entire tape path frequently, using only the suggested materials (pure denatured alcohol, chamois cloth, liquid freon solution). Rub gently, using a horizontal motion, so the cloth doesn't shred and stick to the heads; use chamois-tipped sticks only once so dirt isn't transferred back. Do not use cotton-tipped swabs.

• Clean lenses in a circular motion with lens paper. Do not use handkerchiefs, tissues, fingers or silicone-treated cloths. Clean the plastic monitor face with suggested materials.

• Demagnetize the VTR periodically. Be certain not to touch the video heads (put a layer or two of plastic electrical tape on the demagnetizer to avoid scratching the heads) and withdraw the demagnetizer slowly from the machine.

• Never force anything (10 pin and 8 pin connectors are especially vulnerable to damage). Do not drop, bend or pull cable connections (causing loose wires within the plugs or misaligned plugs); store them in an orderly manner by wrapping rather than twisting or knotting. Wrap in the direction cables naturally want to coil.

• Tighten parts that may have become loose, including the carrying case handle.

• Check all connections for continuity—operate in record and playback modes and wiggle each connector at the point of connection. Alterations in sound or image indicate loose connections.

• Check alignment; play an old tape and look for changes. Check that the take-up reel is operating properly; be certain the cover isn't pressing against any parts; recheck procedures.

• Tape cables that don't have to be moved to the floor; tape microphone and camera cables to the strap on the carrying case, leaving some slack between the case and connections, to prevent connections from loosening.

• Check the power supply and charge batteries after every shooting. Batteries discharge more rapidly in cold weather.

• Wait for the tape to come to a complete stop before changing modes.

• Keep the VTR off the floor and cover it when not in use; rest the camera on its side. Close down and cover its lens.

TABLE E.3: Troubleshooting

Problem	Probable Cause
Visual	
No picture on camera viewfinder.	Lens covered; VTR not in standby mode (press both *Play* and *Record* buttons); f stop closed down completely (turn ring on lens); input selector on VTR not set on *Camera*; VTR not warmed up (allow 10 seconds). Be certain *Video Out* on camera is plugged into *Camera In* on VTR. On studio decks, be certain video gain control is not set on manual or set at zero.
No picture on playback, or gray screen with or without sound.	Check for misthreading; check connections (try different cables); input on monitor set at *TV*—switch to *VTR* mode; adjust brightness and contrast on monitor. Play a tape that was recorded when everything was functioning to locate source of problem. (If the tape plays back, the trouble is in the record process).
Occasional complete loss of picture.	Poor video connection; clogged heads due to inferior tape or low head penetration.
General instability or rolls.	Misthreading; inferior or damaged tape.
Generally noisy picture during playback.	Clogged heads; inferior tape; low head penetration; low-level record current (check power); video level too low (not enough light). Play a previously recorded tape that had a clean image. If noise (snow) appears, check for dirty heads, dirty lens or poor connections. Be certain heads are making contact with tape; brushes (which pass the video current to and from the heads) are clean and straight (tape can be caught in the housing, thereby bending the brushes); and threading is correct.
Picture partially replaced by a snow pattern, horizontally distributed, which stays in the same place (may vary from single lines to most of the picture).	Improper threading; one damaged head; dirty brushes or brushes not making contact.
Dropouts	Dirt, grease, wrinkled tape, lack of iron oxide on tape.
Small black streaks running across scan lines.	Brush noise—similar to dropout, but appears regularly on the same portion of the screen. Clean brushes.
Intermittent black flashes on picture, sometimes with picture breakup.	Dropouts caused by inferior tape or insufficient head penetration.
Black and white streaks across screen that don't appear in the same place when tape is played again.	Slip rings need cleaning.

Visual

Symptom	Cause / Remedy
One or two bars of noise (horizontal bars which move up the picture).	Mistracking owing to incorrectly set tracking control (playback head not aligned with record track) or mechanical guides; capstan servo off lock; damage on edge of tape.
Blurry picture, flickering, poor quality, difficulty focusing, tapes that don't track.	Low voltage from battery or AC line (motors not getting enough power, decreasing tape speed). Recharge battery; reduce number of appliances plugged in.
Clear picture to start; noise increases and gradually replaces picture.	Inferior tape or dirty heads.
Poor image and sound on playback television using RF adapter.	RF unit should be switched to VTR, television on correct channel, and RF cable attached to VHF antenna inputs.
Hooking at top of picture.	Tension controls off.
Squiggly lines or moiré pattern.	Electrical interference from power lines or broadcast stations; defective cable; RF unit overmodulating (wrap with electrical tape).
Serration of picture a few lines wide.	Adust tracking control.
Low frequency beat pattern.	Poor erasure caused by clogged erase heads or low drive.
Sync loss.	Misthreading (be certain tape is passed on inside of tape guide—between the capstan and guide).
Tape wound around capstan.	Common with the portapak—whenever possible, keep the VTR level. Be certain that when the top of the deck is closed it isn't rubbing against the supply reel.

Audio

Symptom	Cause / Remedy
No sound.	Check cables (firmly anchored, not cracked or broken or missing screws). Check audio connection between VTR and monitor; check monitor audio control; clean audio head. Microphone not switched on, plugged in or plugged in fully. Audio level down or not on AGC (studio decks).
Buzz, hum or weak sound.	Audio cables not shielded or properly grounded; nearby electronic gear (car engines, power tools, fluorescent lights) causing interference. Connect cases of all audio equipment by wire (each piece tends to build up its own voltage resulting in different grounds) or connect each piece to the wall outlet with a three-prong AC plug or three-to-two prong adapter and ground wire (attaches to screw on wall plate). Mismatched impedance (microphone

Audio

Picking up radio stations on soundtrack. / does not match VTR impedance); use of high impedance microphone more than 20 feet from VTR. (Use a high to low transformer and add low impedance cables.)

Shielding in wire broken; connections in plug poor.

Playback level low. / Record level low; clogged head, no bias, faulty connector.

Distortion. / Record level too high; incorrect bias, damaged tape edge, poor head-to-tape pressure.

Clogged head, bias too high, poor head-to-tape pressure.

Poor high frequency response.

Wow or flutter. / Bent spool, capstan dirty or worn, servo off lock.

Mechanical

Oscillating pitch. / The equipment normally has a steady hum and high-pitched whistle; a change in or oscillating pitch may indicate head servo trouble.

Brushing noise. / Bent spool.

Squeal. / Excessive tape tension.

Rumble. / Worn motor.

AFTERWORD

The potential uses of television as a learning resource have only begun to be realized. When integrated with various subject areas, video enables students to express themselves; to investigate other students' feelings, the elements of communication and the uses and misuses of technology; to discover ways of effecting positive change; and to use television as a humanizing force and an art form.

Educators no longer need to be concerned about which areas can be taught with video tape, but about using it most effectively within those areas. This does not mean starting from prescriptive studio techniques guaranteed to lead to uniform products, but starting from the learner, school and community as resources for innovation and creative application. Television cannot create magic by itself—what appears before your eyes depends upon the skills of the magician. We delight in magical illusions when we ask to be manipulated, but the electronic emissions emanating from the tube leave us deceived without any expressed desire on our part to be so. Informed "magicians" know how to use their techniques for a positive purpose, and how those same techniques can be used against them. Using video in the classroom helps students understand and control the medium to see through the illusions while retaining all the magic and original fascination.

SELECTED BIBLIOGRAPHY

Books

Anderson, Chuck. *The Electric Journalist: An Introduction to Video.* New York: Praeger, 1973.

Battcock, Gregory, ed. *New Artists Video: A Critical Anthology.* New York: E.P. Dutton, 1978.

Bensinger, Charles. *The Home Video Handbook.* Santa Barbara, CA: Video-Info Publications, 1978.

Bensinger, Charles. *The Video Guide.* 2nd ed. Santa Barbara, CA: Video-Info Publications, 1979.

Benthall, Jonathan, and Ted Polhemus, eds. *The Body as a Medium of Expression.* New York: E.P. Dutton, 1975.

Birdwhistell, Ray L. *Kinesics and Context: Essays on Body Motion Communication.* Philadelphia, PA: University of Pennsylvania Press, 1970.

Bretz, Rudy. *Techniques of Television Production.* 2nd ed. New York: McGraw-Hill, 1962.

Brown, George Isaac. *Human Teaching for Human Learning: An Introduction to Confluent Education.* New York: Viking Press, 1971.

Brown, George Isaac, ed. *The Live Classroom: Innovation Through Confluent Education and Gestalt.* New York: Viking Press, 1975.

Brown, James W., Richard B. Lewis and Fred F. Harcleroad. *Audiovisual Instruction: Technology, Media and Methods.* 5th ed. New York: McGraw-Hill, 1977.

Bunyan, John A., James C. Crimmins and N. Kyri Watson. *Practical Video: The Manager's Guide to Applications.* White Plains, NY: Knowledge Industry Publications, Inc., 1978.

Burrows, Thomas D., and Donald N. Wood. *Television Production: Disciplines and Techniques.* Dubuque, IA: William C. Brown Co., 1978.

Christensen, J.A. *Coping with Television: Teacher's Manual.* Evanston, IL: McDougal, Littell and Co., 1974.

Christensen, J.A. and Curtis Crotty. *Coping with the Mass Media: Teacher's Manual.* Evanston, IL: McDougal, Littell and Co., 1972.

Coming to our senses: The significance of the arts for American education. New York: McGraw-Hill, 1977.

Efrein, Joel Lawrence. *Video Production and Communication Techniques.* Summit, PA: Tab Books, 1971.

Ellis, Elmo I. *Opportunities in Broadcasting.* Skokie, IL: VGM Career Horizons/National Textbook Co., 1977.

Fang, I.E. *Television News.* 2nd ed. New York: Hastings House, 1972.

Garcia, Anthony, and Robert Myers. *Analogies: A Visual Approach to Writing.* New York: McGraw-Hill, 1974.

Gattegno, Caleb. *Towards a Visual Culture.* New York: Discus Books/Avon, 1971.

Gordon, George N. *Classroom Television: New Frontiers in ITV*. New York: Hastings House, 1970.

Hall, Edward T. *The Hidden Dimension: Man's Use of Space in Public and Private*. London: The Bodley Head, Ltd., 1966.

Hall, Mark W. *Broadcast Journalism: An Introduction to News Writing*. New York: Hastings House, 1978.

Harwood, Don. *Video as a Second Language*. New York: VTR Publishing Co., 1975.

Hawley, Robert C., and Isabel L. Hawley. *Developing Human Potential: A Handbook of Activities for Personal and Social Growth*. Amherst, MA: ERA Press, 1975.

Hennings, Dorothy Grant. *Mastering Classroom Communication: What Interaction Analysis Tells the Teacher*. Pacific Palisades, CA: Goodyear, 1975.

Herman, Lewis. *A Practical Manual of Screen Playwriting: for theater and television films*. Cleveland, OH: Forum Books/World Publishing Co., 1963.

Herschensohn, Bruce. *The Gods of Antenna*. New Rochelle, NY: Arlington House, 1976.

Hilgard, Ernest R., and Gordon H. Bower. *Theories of Learning*. Englewood Cliffs, NJ: Prentice-Hall, 1975.

Jennings, Sue. *Remedial Drama*. New York: Theatre Arts Books, 1974.

Kennedy, Keith. *Film Making in Creative Teaching*. New York: Watson-Guptill, 1972.

King, Nancy. *Theatre Movement: The Actor and His Space*. New York: Drama Book Specialists/Publishers, 1971.

Kontos, Peter G., and James J. Murphy, eds. *Teaching Urban Youth: A Source Book for Urban Education*. New York: John Wiley and Sons, 1967.

Laybourne, Kit, and Pauline Cianciolo, eds. *Doing the Media*. New York: McGraw-Hill, 1978.

Linton, Dolores, and David Linton. *Practical Guide to Classroom Media*. Dayton, OH: Pflaum/Standard, 1971.

Littell, Joseph Fletcher, ed. *Coping with the Mass Media*. Evanston, IL: McDougal, Littell and Co., 1972.

Littell, Joseph Fletcher, ed. *Coping with Television*. Evanston, IL: McDougal, Littell and Co., 1973.

Lyon, Harold C. Jr. *Learning to Feel—Feeling to Learn: Humanistic Education for the Whole Man*. Columbus, OH: Charles E. Merrill, 1971.

Mankiewicz, Frank, and Joel Swerdlow. *Remote Control: Television and the Manipulation of American Life*. New York: Ballantine Books, 1978.

Mattingly, Grayson, and Welby Smith. *Introducing the Single-Camera VTR System: A Layman's Guide to Videotape Recording*. New York: Charles Scribner's Sons, 1973.

Maynard, Richard A. *The Celluloid Curriculum*. New York: Hayden, 1971.

Mehrabian, Albert. *Public Places and Private Spaces: The Psychology of Work, Play, and Living Environments*. New York: Basic Books, 1976.

Millerson, Gerald. *The Technique of Television Production*. 9th ed. New York: Hastings House, 1972.

Millerson, Gerald. *TV Camera Operation.* New York: Hastings House, 1973.

Montgomery, Chandler. *Art for Teachers of Children: Foundations of Aesthetic Experience.* Columbus, OH: Charles E. Merrill Publishing Co., 1968.

Morrow, James, and Murray Suid. *Media and Kids: Real-World Learning in the Schools.* Rochelle Park, NJ: Hayden Book Co., Inc., 1977.

Murray, Michael. *The Videotape Book: A Basic Guide to Portable TV Production for Families, Friends, Schools and Neighborhoods.* New York: Bantam Books, 1975.

Norback, Peter, and Craig Norback, eds. *Great Songs of Madison Avenue.* New York: Quadrangle/ The New York Times Book Company, 1976.

Parsons, Theodore W. *Guided Self-Analysis System for Professional Development Education Series.* Berkeley, CA: 2140 Shattuck Avenue, 1971.

Parsons, Theodore W., William Tikunoff and Patricia M. Cabrera. *Achieving Classroom Communication Through Self Analysis.* Studio City, CA: Prismatica International, Inc., 1973.

Price, Jonathan. *Video-Visions: A Medium Discovers Itself.* New York: Plume/New American Library, 1977.

Rissover, Frederic, and David C. Birch, eds. *Mass Media and the Popular Arts.* New York: McGraw-Hill, 1972.

Robinson, J.F., and P.H. Beards. *Using Videotape.* New York: Focal Press/Hastings House, 1976.

Robinson, Richard. *The Video Primer.* New York: Links Books, 1974.

Rogovin, Mark, Marie Burton and Holly Highfill. *Mural Manual: How to Paint Murals for the Classroom, Community Center and Street Corner.* Boston: Beacon Press, 1973.

Rosen, Stephen. *Future Facts: A Forecast of the World as We Will Know It Before the End of the Century.* New York: Simon and Schuster, 1976.

Ruesch, Jurgen, and Weldon Kees. *Nonverbal Communication: Notes on the Visual Perception of Human Relations.* Berkeley, CA: University of California Press, 1970.

Schneider, Ira, and Beryl Korot, eds. *Video Art: An Anthology.* New York: Harcourt Brace Jovanovich, 1976.

Schrank, Jeffrey. *Teaching Human Beings: 101 Subversive Activities for the Classroom.* Boston: Beacon Press, 1972.

Schrank, Jeffrey, ed. *TV Action Book.* Evanston, IL: McDougal, Littell and Co., 1974.

Schrank, Jeffrey. *Using Mass Media.* Skokie, IL: National Textbook Co., 1975.

Schwartz, Tony. *The Responsive Chord.* New York: Anchor Press/Doubleday, 1973.

Seaberg, Dorothy I. *The Four Faces of Teaching: The Role of the Teacher in Humanizing Education.* Pacific Palisades, CA: Goodyear Publishing Co., Inc., 1974.

Shaftel, Fannie R., and George Shaftel. *Role-Playing for Social Values: Decision-Making in the Social Studies.* Englewood Cliffs, NJ: Prentice-Hall, 1967.

Shawn, Ted. *Every Little Movement: A Book About François Delsarte.* New York: Dance Horizons, 1963.

Sommer, Robert. *Personal Space: The Behavioral Basis of Design.* Englewood Cliffs, NJ: Prentice-Hall, 1969.

Spiegel, John P., and Pavel Machotka. *Messages of the Body.* New York: Free Press/Macmillan, 1974.

Spolin, Viola. *Improvisation for the Theater.* Evanston, IL: Northwestern University Press, 1963.

Stasheff, Edward, and Rudy Bretz. *The Television Program: Its Direction and Production.* 4th ed. New York: Hill and Wang, 1968.

Stewig, John W. *Spontaneous Drama: A Language Art.* Columbus, OH: Charles E. Merrill, 1973.

Stevens, John O. *Awareness: Exploring, Experimenting, Experiencing.* Moab, UT: Real People Press, 1971.

Toffler, Alvin, ed. *Learning for Tomorrow: The Role of the Future in Education.* New York: Vintage Books, 1974.

Valdes, Joan, and Jeanne Crow, eds. *The Media Reader.* Dayton, OH: Pflaum, 1975.

Valdes, Joan, and Jeanne Crow. *The Media Works.* Dayton, OH: Pflaum, 1973.

Videofreex. *The Spaghetti City Video Manual.* New York: Praeger Publishers, 1973.

Way, Brian. *Development through Drama.* London: Longman, 1967.

Weiner, Peter. *Making the Media Revolution: A Handbook for Video-Tape Production.* New York: Macmillan, 1973.

Weinland, Thomas P., and Donald W. Protheroe. *Social Science Projects You Can Do.* Englewood Cliffs, NJ: Prentice-Hall, 1973.

Youngblood, Gene. *Expanded Cinema.* New York: E.P. Dutton, 1970.

Zettl, Herbert. *Television Production Handbook.* 3rd ed. Belmont, CA: Wadsworth Publishing Co., Inc., 1976.

Zettl, Herbert. *Television Production Workbook.* 3rd ed. Belmont, CA: Wadsworth Publishing Co., Inc., 1977.

Periodicals

Ackerman, Amy S. "Media Pals: A Cultural Exchange Project." *Audiovisual Instruction,* September 1977.

Allender, Robert and Jay Yanoff. "Using Video for Teacher (and Student) Training." *Media and Methods,* October 1977.

Bender, Eileen T. "Cable TV: Road to Where?" *Media and Methods,* October 1978.

Bryer, Judith Eve. "Video Pen Pals Say 'Aloha'." *Learning,* December 1975.

Cabeceiros, James. "A Cure for Multiple Video-itis." *Audiovisual Instruction,* September 1976.

Chotzen, Yvonne Elisabeth. "Videotape Verité in the Study Process." *Audiovisual Instruction.* March 1977.

Douglass, Richard L., et al. "Develop Your Own Mediated Career Information." *Audiovisual Instruction,* April 1976.

DuBey, Kenneth. "How to Videotape Through a Microscope." *Audiovisual Instruction,* January 1978.

Eanet, Alan S., and Sandra M. Toth. "Using TV in a Science Course." *Audiovisual Instruction,* March 1976.

Gerard, Helene. "The Past is Still Present." *Media and Methods,* November 1977.

Grady, Michael P. "Students Need Media for a Balanced Brain." *Audiovisual Instruction,* April 1976.

Hawkins, Sue. "Tape Record Your Teaching: A Step-by-Step Approach." *Learning Resources,* April 1975.

Hessler, Don. "Using Television Commercials in the Classroom." Los Angeles Unified School District Instructional Planning Division, KLCS-Channel 58. (No date. Mimeo.)

Holt, David. "Very Special Students, Very Special Video." *Media and Methods,* January 1978.

Horsman, Maurine. "Can Video Bring Happiness to a 16mm Film Production?" *Audiovisual Instruction,* January 1975.

Jay, M. Ellen. "Student Interviews With Celebrities." *Audiovisual Instruction,* September 1976.

Jones, Robert B. "How to Write Successful ITV Scripts." *Audiovisual Instruction,* May 1976.

Kaplan, Don. "How to Tickle a Whale and Other Everyday Activities." *Music Educators Journal* 64 (October 1977).

Kaplan, Don. "The Joys of Noise: Part One." *Music Educators Journal* 62 (February 1976).

Kaplan, Don. "The Joys of Noise: Part Two." *Music Educators Journal* 62 (March 1976).

LeBaron, John and Louise Kanne. "Child-created Television in the Inner City." *The Elementary School Journal* 75 (April 1975).

Mack, Theresa. "How to Live Without a Father: The Making of a Videodrama." *Teachers and Writers Collaborative Newsletter,* Spring 1975.

Mueller, Lavonne. "The Mask." *Media and Methods,* February 1977.

Pinto, Robert. "What To Do When Your Portapak Doesn't." *Educational and Industrial Television,* October 1974.

Potter, Rosemary Lee. "TV Week: A Special Program of Events." *Teacher,* January 1979.

Powell, Jon T. "Buying Video Equipment—A Guide for the Thrifty." *Media and Methods,* October 1977.

Radical Software. Special issue on "Video and Kids," Vol. 2 No. 6.

Sharapan, Hedda B. "Misterogers' Neighborhood: A Resource for Exceptional Children." *Audiovisual Instruction,* February 1973.

Sitton, Thad. "The Fire That Lit Up Learning." *Teacher,* March 1979.

Steenland, Sally. "An Activist Approach to Critical TV Viewing." *Media and Methods,* November 1977.

Stoltz, Jack. "Teaching with TV Commercials." *Educational and Industrial Television,* October 1978.

Thompson, Mary Langer. "Symbolic Immortality: A New Approach to the Study of Death." *Media and Methods,* February 1977.

Travis, Rosemary L. "The Language of the Body." *Media and Methods,* September 1977.

Wigginton, Eliot. "The Foxfire Approach: it can work for you." *Media and Methods,* November 1977.

Willis, Meredith Sue. "Fiction Scripts for Film and Video." *Teachers and Writers Collaborative Newsletter,* Spring 1975.

Wynn, Danny M. and Bruce W. Craig. "You Can Turn Your Students into Subject Matter Specialists!" *Audiovisual Instruction,* February 1978.

GLOSSARY

AC/DC Converter: Device that converts alternating current (AC) into direct current (DC); used to drive a portapak.

Action: Any performance in front of a camera.

Ad Lib: Spontaneous speech or action.

AGC: Automatic Gain Control: Automatic volume or picture adjustment.

ALC: Automatic Light Control: Automatic adjustment of lens opening.

Ambient Sound: Natural, environmental sound that adds presence and depth.

Amplifier: Device that magnifies electronic signals.

Arc: Curving truck, pan and dolly movement around a subject.

Aspect Radio: Proportional ratio of television screen width to height (4:3).

Assemble Edit: Process of shooting scenes out of sequence, then assembling them in the desired order.

Audio: Sound portion of a television production.

Audio Head: Electromagnet that records, reads and erases sound.

Backspacing Editing System: Device that backs up the video tape when the camera is stopped, preventing a glitch from occurring.

Barn Door: Flat piece of metal used to adjust the parameters of a light's beam.

Beta Format: Popular video cassette format, pioneered by Sony Corporation.

Blanking: Moment when the scanning beam retraces its path before scanning another line.

Boom: Device incorporating a long arm for suspending a microphone.

Bridge: Material providing a transition from one scene to another (e.g., a musical bridge).

Burn-In: Camera tube image retention caused by aiming the camera at a high-contrast source such as a bright light.

Camera Angle: Angle of the camera in relation to the subject (e.g., high, low, oblique).

Canted Shot: Shot in which subjects appear to tilt toward one of the upper corners of the frame, usually used to convey an emotional state.

Cassette: Audio or video tape format enclosing both supply and take-up reels in a plastic container.

CATV: Community Antenna Television (cable television): Transmission of signals through a coaxial cable from a master antenna to individual television sets.

CCTV: Closed Circuit Television: Direct transmission of signals from camera to monitor/receiver through cables connected to both.

Chroma Key: Electronic matting process used in color television.

Coaxial Cable: Standard camera and video cable.

Condenser Microphone: Sensitive microphone with a wide frequency range, employing a vibrating condenser plate and a fixed back plate.

Continuity Board: Nonverbal, sequenced visualization of narrative or non-narrative action, similar to a comic strip.

Control Track: Portion of video tape used to record the synchronizing pulse.

Cover Shot: Showing the entire action occurring within a large area, often used as an establishing shot.

Crawl: Display moving horizontally or vertically across the screen. Often called a "roll."

Cross-Fade: One audio or video source faded out while the next source is faded in.

Cucalorus: Pattern placed into or in front of a spotlight to create shadow effects on a set or backdrop. Also called "cookie."

Cue: Signal to the talent or technicans.

Cue Card (Idiot Sheet): Large card with material for the talent to read, held next to or just below the camera.

Cutaway: Shot of a peripheral object or scene, often used for transition.

Cutting Ratio: Relative size of an object in two successive shots. An excessive change will disrupt continuity (e.g., cutting from a long shot to an extreme close-up).

Depth of Field: Area that is in focus, determined by focal length, camera/subject distance, and size of aperture.

Depth Staging: Arrangement of foreground and background elements.

Docudrama: Dramatized account of a real event.

Dolly: Physical movement of the camera closer to (dolly in) or farther away from (dolly out) the subject.

Downstage: Close to the audience.

Dropout: Loss of part of the video signal, appearing as streaks or white glitches. Generally caused by dirt or poor quality tape.

Dubbing: 1. Duplication of an electronic recording (tape to tape or record to tape). 2. Erasure of a previously recorded sound track and the addition of a new track.

Dynamic Microphone: Rugged microphone employing a diaphragm connected to a moveable coil.

Electron Gun: Device in the rear of the camera tube which produces the electron scanning beam, "shooting" it onto the photoelectrical surface covering the front of the tube.

Electronic Viewfinder: Small television tube in the back of the camera used as a viewfinder.

Establishing Shot: Shot to orient the viewer and establish a scene.

Fade In/Out: Gradually increase or diminish video or audio.

Field: Half a complete frame, containing alternate scan lines, lasting 1/60 of a second.

Field of View: Scope of a shot.

Flare: Undesirable streaks caused by reflection from a bright light.

Floodlight: Light which produces a broad, diffused beam.

Focal Length: Distance between the optical center point of the lens and area upon which the image is focused. Generally classified as normal (approximating actual viewer distance), short (wide angle), and long (telephoto).

Focal Point: Point which the camera is focused upon.

Follow Focus: Process of turning the focusing ring to keep a subject in focus during subject or camera movement.

Format: 1. Framework of a program. 2. Width of video tape.

Frame: 1. One complete picture consisting of two fields, lasting 1/30 of a second. 2. Composition of elements within the television frame (e.g., positioning a subject close to the borders to create a "tight" frame, or with a large amount of space between the subject and the borders to create a "loose" frame).

Framed Shot: Framing a subject with parts of a person or object.

Freeze Frame: Stop action on a single frame.

Fresnel Spotlight: Common spotlight with an adjustable beam and stepped lens.

f-Stop: Term used to describe various apertures (sizes of iris openings in the lens). The larger the opening, the small the f-stop number.

Gaffers Tape: Strong tape used for attaching electrical fixtures.

Gain: 1. Audio volume. Adjusting the sound level is referred to as "riding gain." 2. Strength of television picture (contrast).

Generation: A copy or dub of a tape or film.

Ghosting: Undesirable double image caused by signal reflections, usually from tall buildings.

Glitch: Roll, often accompanying a change of shot or scene as the video heads are brought up to speed.

Gobo: A scenic foreground placed several feet in front of the camera, integrating with the background action.

Graphic: Two-dimensional visual—titles, maps, charts, graphs, etc.

Headroom: Space between the top of the subject and the top of the frame.

Helical Scan (Slant-Track): Process whereby video information is recorded on the tape in a helical (slanted-line) pattern.

Hot-Spot: Undesirable concentration of light, common in rear screen projection.

Impedance: Resistance to the flow of an audio signal in a microphone cable. A high impedance microphone uses a long cable.

In-Camera Edit: Process of shooting scenes in sequence.

Incandescent Bulb: Basic source of light, employing a heated filament in a glass bulb.

Inky: Small spotlight.

Insert Edit: Process of inserting new material within material already recorded.

Jump Cut: 1. Two successive shots of the same subject in slightly different positions; the subject appears to "jump" for no apparent reason. 2. Intentionally showing only the beginning and end of a complete action where the intervening action is unnecessary.

Key Light: Main source of illumination for the subject.

Keystone Effect: Distortion in which parallel lines no longer appear parallel, caused by poor camera/graphic placement.

Lavalier: A small microphone worn around the neck or attached to the speaker's clothing. Also spelled "lavaliere."

Lead Room: Additional space on the side of the subject toward which the subject is moving or looking.

Leko (Ellipsoidal) Light: Spotlight with a sharply defined beam that can be focused into rectangular shapes and projected through a cucalorus.

Light Ratio: Relative intensities of key, fill and back lights (usually 1:1:½). The exact ratio changes depending upon varying conditions such as attire and set.

Matte: 1. Foreground or stenciled shape placed over the lens, used in combination with the subject to create a composite image. 2. Electronic effect using two cameras—one with the foreground material, the other with the background material—to create a composite image.

Mike (Mic): Microphone.

Moiré Effect: Wavy lines caused by a narrow striped pattern interacting with the scanning lines.

Monitor: High quality, lightweight television designed for use with a VTR, accepting signals directly from the deck. A monitor/receiver accepts RF signals as well.

Montage: Rapid succession of moving or still images assembled to create an overall effect.

Musique Concrète: Ordinary environmental sounds manipulated on audio tape.

Noise: 1. Audio or video interference (on video, appearing as a "snow" pattern). 2. Interference with the communication process.

Objective Camera Treatment: Method of shooting in which the camera assumes an objective role, merely observing the action.

On Location: Any place outside the studio.

O/S: Over-the-Shoulder Shot: Looking at one subject framed by the back of the head and shoulder of another subject.

Over Exposure: Excessively bright image.

Pan: Camera movement created by pivoting the camera in a lateral direction from a fixed position.

Panning Head: Mechanism on the camera mounting that permits controlled panning and tilting.

Perspective: 1. Audio: Matching audio with video depth. 2. Video: Creating the illusion of depth by using converging lines at a single point on the horizon.

Pic Stand: Lightweight stand for lights.

Pickup Pattern: Pattern of sound heard clearly by a microphone (e.g., cardioid, uni-, bi- or omnidirectional).

Plano-Convex Lens: Basic spotlight lens with one flat and one convex surface.

Plot: Outlined pattern of action taken by a central character or characters involving the exposition, conflict, complications, climax and resolution.

Portapak: Small, portable, lightweight camera and VTR format, intended to be used by one person, which is battery operated and records on ½-inch or ¼-inch tape.

Prompter: Device used to provide talent with simple cues or fully scripted material. Forms range from simple ring binders to sophisticated electronic systems.

Quadraplex: Two-inch professional format using four rotating heads to record video information on tape in a transverse pattern. Also spelled "quadruplex".

Quartz Bulb: Small, powerful light with a stable color temperature generally used for color television, employing a high intensity tungsten-halogen filament in a quartz or silica housing.

Raster: Blank lines created by the deflected beam when there is no input.

Reaction Shot: Shot indicating a character's response.

Rear Screen Projection: Visual projected on a translucent screen from behind, photographed from in front.

Receiver: Home television set accepting RF signals.

Resolution: Clarity and detail of the television picture.

Reveal: Type of graphic produced by instantaneously or gradually exposing its parts.

Reverse Angle Shot: Showing the action from the opposite direction while keeping the camera on the same side of the action.

RF: Radio Frequency: Frequency broadcast through the air shared by television, radio, citizens band, police and other communication services.

RF Converter: Device which enables video tapes to be played back through a receiver.

Rule of Thirds: Principle of composition that divides the screen into thirds, horizontally and vertically, and places important subjects at the points where lines intersect.

Safe Area: Area of the television screen within which all important graphics or action must be framed to be seen.

Scanning: Movement of the electron beam from left to right and from top to bottom in both the camera and receiver. One scan equals one field.

Scoop: Floodlight with a very wide beam.

Segue: Selections of music or other audio following one another without a pause.

Semiscripted Outline: Script format including specific opening and closing action, cues and important dialogue, with the major action ad libbed.

Sequence: A series of scenes.

Servo Capstan: Device on the VTR which pulls the tape through at a constant speed.

Shot: 1. Any uninterrupted length of taped or filmed action. 2. Field of view (long shot, mid shot, close-up, extreme close-up), area of subject visible (e.g., head shot), or number of subjects visible (e.g., two shot).

Shot Sheet: List of shots attached to the back of the camera including types of lens, type of shot and camera movement.

Single Camera System: 1. Production in which one camera records all the action, and shots are edited in-camera or in the post-production process. 2. Simultaneous recording of sound and picture on the same film.

Special Effects Generator: Device which creates electronic effects such as wipes, inserts, keys and split screens, using more than one video input.

Spotlight: Light which projects a precise, directional beam through a lens using a focusing reflector.

Stop Down: Reduce size of lens aperture.

Storyboard: Continuity board indicating action, shot, and (often) audio for a narrative or documentary production.

Subject: Person or object that is the focus of attention.

Subjective Camera Treatment: Method of shooting in which the camera assumes a subjective role, acting as a person or object in the scene.

Sync Pulse: Signal that synchronizes all video components. The horizontal pulse controls the horizontal movement of the scanning beams; the vertical pulse controls the vertical movement.

Talent: Actor or actress.

Talking Heads: Program consisting of conversation or discussion, with no other physical action (e.g., a panel discussion).

Three-Point Lighting: Triangular arrangement of key, fill and backlights.

Tilt: Camera movement up or down from a fixed position.

Tracking: 1. Angle at which the video tape passes the video heads. The heads need to be properly adjusted so that the recording phase matches the playback phase. 2. Another name for trucking.

Transverse Scan: Method used in quadraplex recording where video information is recorded in bands that are almost perpendicular to the length of the tape.

Treatment: Method of portraying the action; style or form of presentation.

Truck: Camera movement parallel to the subject created by moving the camera with its mount (as opposed to panning from a fixed position).

UHF: Ultra High Frequency: Channels 14-83.

Under Exposure: Excessively dark picture.

Upstage: Away from the audience.

VCR: Video Cassette Recorder: Machine which performs the same functions as a VTR, using a cassette format.

VHF: Very High Frequency: Channels 2-13.

VHS: Video Home System: Popular video cassette format and main competitor with the Beta format.

Video: 1. Small format television. 2. Visual portion of a television production.

Video Art: Use of television for its graphic potential rather than its ability to communicate audiovisual information.

Video Feedback: Effect produced by feeding the camera's signal into the monitor while using the same camera to photograph the monitor.

Video Heads: Electromagnets used to record and play back video signals.

Video Tape: Material for storing sound images and control track information electronically, consisting of iron oxide particles on a plastic base, measuring ¼ inch to 2 inches in width.

Video Verite: Anthropological approach intended to record an event without manipulation or preconceptions.

Vidicon Tube: Basic camera pickup tube.

VO: Voice Over:Narration or dialogue added, during post-production, over an existing soundtrack.

VTR: Video Tape Recorder: Magnetic/electronic recording machine.

VU Meter: Volume Unit Meter: Device used to visually register sound levels.

Walking Shot: Photographing a subject while walking along with the subject, often used during an interview.

Wash Out: Flattening or fading of picture caused by excessive lighting.

Whizz (Swish Pan): Rapid pan, blurring intermediate detail.

Wind Screen: Device (usually foam rubber) used over a microphone during outdoor recording to reduce the sound of wind and other environmental noises.

Zoom Lens: Lens which changes focal length from telephoto to wide angle.

INDEX

ABOUT THE AUTHOR

Don Kaplan has more than 10 years' experience in instructional design for the visual and performing arts in elementary, graduate, adult and special education settings. Currently Sensory Development Instructor at the Center for Independent Living, New York Infirmary, he has taught arts-in-education at the Bank Street College of Education and other colleges, and various arts classes at elementary and senior high schools in New York City.

Mr. Kaplan has written articles on film, TV, music, art, dance and theater for magazines including *Media and Methods, Music Educators Journal* and *Teaching*. He is a contributor to *Doing the Media* (McGraw-Hill) and Video Editor of the *Film Library Quarterly*. He holds a B.S. in Music Education from Hunter College and an M.A. in Creative Arts from New York University.

THE AUTHOR